LOVE DISTINGUISHED - SERIES THREE

THE HEART *of* Love

APMI Publications
a division of Alan Pateman Ministries
P.O. Box 17,
55051 Barga (LU),
Tuscany, Italy

❖

Books
BY AGENE JUSTICE ONOTIEMORIA

1. Love
2. The Wonderland of Love
3. The Heart of Love
4. Sweet Bitter Love
5. Stolen Love

AVAILABLE FROM APMI PUBLICATIONS,
AMAZON.COM AND OTHER RETAIL OUTLETS

LOVE DISTINGUISHED - SERIES THREE

THE HEART of Love

AGENE JUSTICE ONOTIEMORIA

❖

BOOK 3 OF A 5 BOOK SERIES
Love Distinguished

BOOK TITLE: **The Heart of Love**
Book Series, Love Distinguished 3 of 5

WRITTEN BY AGENE JUSTICE ONOTIEMORIA
Paperback ISBN: 978-1-909132-31-3
eBook ISBN: 978-1-909132-16-0

Published By:
APMI Publications
In Partnership with Truth for the Journey Books
Email: publications@alanpatemanministries.com
www.AlanPatemanMinistries.com

Acknowledgements:
Cover Design Copyright APMI
Senior Editor/Publisher: Dr. Alan Pateman
Editing/Proofreading/Research: Dr. Jennifer Pateman
Computer Administration/Office Manager: Dr. Dorothea Struhlik
Cover Image Credit: www.PosterMyWall.com

Unless otherwise indicated, all scriptural quotations are from the King James Version of the bible.

*Where scriptures appear with special emphasis (**in bold,** italic or <u>underlined</u>) we have edited them ourselves in order to bring focused attention within the context of this subject being taught.*

❖

Dedication

I dedicate this book to my unquestionable God, who saw me as a worthy fountain pen to reach the world. I dedicate it to my biological brothers and sisters, both at home and abroad, including my parents who always keep up with their support, you are my backbone. In addition my mentors and benefactors, well done, let's work together as a team for solid achievement. I also dedicate this work to all of my well-wishers, pastors, brethren and friends, whether home or abroad your "Hi," means a lot to me. Keep it up. God bless you all.

❖

Table of Contents

❖

CHAPTER 1

Homosexual Lovers

Beyond what is Normal

These are people who over lust for people by having them attracted to them too much, such that is beyond normal. It could be women or even men. They can stay on their own and ejaculate by merely looking at a picture or imagine the nudity of a lady physically, even without being naked.

They mostly love men instead of women, as God created it. The majority of them are suffering from it, as a result of attacks from this dark world, assigned by Satanic agents just to mess them up.

It could be sacrifice for occult practices over one or two things. What else would they use to lay claim as to why they are just doing this, other than money? Whereby many are actually desperate when it comes to wealth issues. I don't want to take it like that. And I cannot accept that popular attribute by many.

Observationally, many are homosexual due to the environment in which they found themselves, whereby women could be too expensive, where they have no money to always have them on their sides. Apart from that, some men do dream of ladies like mugs, and begin to hide and seek, by keep burning in passion without even expressing their feelings. The bible says, our thoughts assail us (Heb 2:18).

Resigned to their Imaginations

They have another problem with shortness of words, relating to toasting and yearning for a woman. Look, if you don't use the appropriate register of any animal to it, it can never answer you the way you want. As they just don't know how, rather they simply resign to imaginations and as the action of imagination is going on within them, immediately, they ejaculate and even be released.

In short, it is a curse on any man in this situation. And without deliverance, no one can avert it except God. Whenever they are bathing, they must use soap to massage until they release, otherwise they can never agree to be bathed. The secret is that impersonator in the second life of human beings make their urge become so very high beyond their normal control, that is why.

This is commonly noticed among single students in the wide world. Masturbation is the order of their days just for them to be able to go far in their pursuits and as well as to protect their careers. Such men hardly like women. There could also be the situation whereby a particular section of a blue-film, it's required that one must do this and since it is money, one is forced to do it.

There is no normal human being on earth that will just deliberately choose to be doing this except he is possessed by evil spirits.

Population Reduction

Any man who does this all by himself becomes more violent due to lack of joy. Some do it as a result of fear of brethren of the same religion with them. As the culture of religion or church states that those who worship God must be holy for God is holy (1 Pt 1:16).

They resign to doing it by hide and seek. The number one disadvantage here is that, since the men doing this cannot multiply by reproduction through mating, (as they hate women), the devil has succeeded in reducing the number of the population on earth.

❖

CHAPTER 2

Bisexual Lovers

Even Animals can Differentiate

These are men who are in love with men, by engaging in sex with them. It is very sad and piteous that even a common animal in the business can differentiate between a male or female animal by carefully sniffing its anus before deciding to embark on sex with it. But in the case of these people, the reverse is the case. They are no longer partial about women, if at all. They are some how accursed and as a result they are voluntary workers actually working for Satan.

Probably they have been enticed, out of a desire for wealth and therefore resign themselves to bisexual acts. Alternatively, they could say, "Will you rather prefer that every man sleeps with your wife?" Since he love his wife, he will gladly do without impulsive. If you cannot avoid a particular thing there is every atom that you must endure it.

You know it is an abomination to sleep with your same blood person by sex and so, in order to avoid it, you will be forced to do this. And that with this alone, you have safeguarded your family against spiritual intruders.

Similarly, it could be so much hard on you that all the single ladies eventually got angry and so ganged up against you such that you can have no choice than to pass through this process in order to get what you actually yearn for in there. Bisexuality has long been started. From centuries, it is being an evil activity practiced by some elements and even being introduced into human system in our society.

The Land of Sodom and Gomorrah

God purposely destroyed the land of Sodom and Gomorrah as a result of this. It has helped to calm some of their agents completely down, among men extraordinarily handsome with some attraction just for this purpose. If you really take a critical look at some men, they are like angels, but go to their background, you will see something disgustful.

God created a married man and a married woman that when both of them mate — fulfil their individual legal rightful obligations towards each other — it results in a foetus, which by the grace of the God and based on His ordination, will result in offspring.

However due to some humanly considered expenses, compounded with the inability to toast or talk to any freed lady on the basis of expressing one's emotional feelings toward her — until one is accepted — one resigns to bisexuality because fellow men are cheap for one to easily talk to or relate with, without any form of shyness.

Secondly, some guys are fond with sissy, which provoke someone to do undo. If he just cannot afford having himself being called a womaniser, will gape at women and become much closer to men. Before you know it, it will become even much difficult for him to relate with women. Spirit of timidity has so much dealt with some men to the extent they can't even voice their feelings any more on the basis of this situation.

Occult Practices

Occult practices involve the spiritual realm. And so, if they say, this is what you must do, it is compulsory that you will definitely obey without any atom of disobedience. If you are doing a dirty job like blue-films or even prostitution and you happen to fall due to this category, you are bound by oath to. They can transfer spirit from here to someone or even exchange spirits when they are tired.

Women make a man to become soft. But since these sets of people do not often mate with women or not at all, they become much more violent. God said we should multiply. As they don't give to women, they just can't multiply, hence reduction in population of man on the earth becomes the order of the day because they are wasting the semen.

So many students indulge in it in order to protect their careers else if they impregnate any lady, their parents can no longer be responsible for their school fees.

❖

CHAPTER 3

Heterosexual Love

Attracted to the Opposite Sex

It is a situation whereby a person is sexually attracted to people especially of the opposite sex. This is usually not ordinary if you are spiritually inclined. A deliverance minister can tell you much about this. You will be surprised to hear what you don't even think can happen, not to talk of existing in this entire world. God will deliver us because the world is truly dangerous in the hand of mankind.

For demonic business to be lucrative among men, it takes a lovely attractive something to be able to get the attention of human beings. Human beings like anything that is beautiful; whether fake or original, they don't care to know, provided it carries their desirable colour. This is where the devil easily get humans into his ministries.

In the kingdom of darkness, a lady who wants to meet extra men for her bad job, can go as far as buying shape from the corresponding office in there. And this time, no eyes will ever pass her by without taking a second look at her. And in second look, some emotional feelings must spring up in the heart of the man and that of course marks the beginning of her advantage.

Major Target Areas

There are four major targeted areas of a woman by men. Number one, her facial look, is she beautiful? If yes, she has waned percentages. Number two, does she have moderate or big breasts? If yes, she has also got the expected kind of woman by men. The third stage is, does she have a big or moderate bonbon? The last but not the least stage is her complete shape. Does she have a good shape? If yes, she has gotten 60% and that is fine.

The rest are just minor things, which can only be seen after taking off her clothes. Furthermore, characters, smoking or not, drinking or not, clubbing or not, outdoor or indoor personality or not etc., are to be verified here after.

Back to the crux, in a nutshell, if a lady is possessed with any power concerning sexual attraction by men, she risks her matrimony, if care is not taken she may never marry all her life. Every man that sees her would want to make love to her. Since she is a material to the demons, they may not even want her to settle down with a permanent husband. They will consider a husband to be a kind of disturbance to her mission. For her mission is to drag men to the mound.

She can be sent to wreck anyone completely down. She could be sent to initiate and collect blood and semen from some targeted fellows. To the ignorant, they are very beautiful, in that there's no man who doesn't want them. In short, they are even the ones now selecting the ones they accept to even talk to with, without knowing the future implication of this demonic gift.

There is nothing like the natural blessing from the Lord God, which adds no sorrow. The bible says: "The blessing of the LORD, it maketh rich, and he addeth no sorrow with it" (Prv 10:22 KJV). Therefore, if you are a lady under this kind of influence—having gifts with demonic powers—then I suggest you go for a total deliverance, else you're in trouble.

Only to Lose their Souls

It will come to a time in a man's life where even his or her age will begin to decline. In that case, if you did not lay a good foundation for yourself, just begin to consider yourself with a dramatic case. For how long can one continue seeking to gain the whole world, only to lose their soul? Remember life is not forever. At a time, someone must plan and arrange him or herself well; otherwise it will be too rough in the prospect.

In this scenario, I would love someone to use his or her initiative for good. In some issues, there is no way one can bite and chew for you, especially when you have your own teeth.

❖

CHAPTER 4

Love of Blue-Films

A Dirty kind of Job

These are films acted by people doing some dirty kind of jobs like sex films. They are highly aided because it is a bloody job by the concerned people. As everybody wants to be rich overnight, the lazy ones do not mind what they do in order to get money.

After all, money doesn't voice where on earth it was gotten or made. And as such, many are covered with that confidence. Their focus is to balance the equation of financial breakthrough with every other person, whether equal, above or even beneath.

The major purpose for the film is to initiate people, in order to harvest souls for the kingdom in charge of it, in the ministry of the devil. Secondly, it is also to teach people all kinds of sex styles in the act. It wants to tell you that you can catch fun in sex.

Demons always want Blood

When you are watching the films, they can help to develop your urge into the main action with readiness to perform. It is used on drug business. Demons are responsible for all this, because it's through this that they can also get blood. It seduces people through their mind set, particularly those that watch.

When you are watching the film, it stimulates your complete sexual urge. It makes you see details about so many ladies. Some can even climax or release as the case maybe and that depends on the individual.

Any blue-film actor or actress might not marry, his or her entire life. When you over view ladies on this aspect, you could hate them and so settle down with one that's disgustful to you and even switch your interest under probability. This I tell you has created opportunity for men to enjoy different women with different sizes of privates and as well as women to enjoy different men with different sizes of privates also.

Above all, even collectively, they are simply instruments for Satan to corrupt the world. God is just too merciful if we all should consider the atrocities of men in this world. May God deliver us and have mercy, in Jesus' name.

CHAPTER 5

Under 18 Lovers

Sleeping with Children

Dealing with one's mate in love or sex is okay but not as far as sleeping with children you worth to be their father or even grandfather or even running along with small boys of your son's age-mate. An adult that had indulged in this act, has reported that it is like a child playing on top of the mother and father and meanwhile doing and enjoying the quiet moment in the act.

It was also gathered that, they are less expensive and hardly can take in. And so for that reason, you can hardly detect or suspect that something related is going on between them.

Ignorantly for the young ones in question, they are used for intelligent rituals. Similarly, for the adults to also be fleshing up their bloods and renew their skins; and if you watch very well, it reflects on their skins and that serves as pleasure to them.

Some of these innocent young generations could be virgin and for that reason if they try them and succeed, that is the end. He or she is being taught. It is a pity. No more slack in the action. The monkey is already aware of the banana. They are easy to maintain with less cost, sex-wise.

Apart from being approached by the adult, the girl or boy could decide by themselves to show appreciation, over numerous assistance from him or her for some time. They are not too dull, compared to adults like them, they said. It is risked, if you are caught anywhere in the world. It is considered a rape-like kind of offence in the human court of law. So, any fellow like that could be charged with child sexual abuse.

Sexually Groomed

Sometimes, even some under 18's usually do grow above their ages with some body attractions, which could instantly stimulate approach on this basis. When he or she is preparing for a future dirty job (blue-film) they must be groomed up beforehand.

It could also be an inherited of something. Secondly, it also can be a curse. Anything outside the will of God, is a mission by Satan. Every person wants any organ, which can match with their own. It could be used to set any targeted fellow up in order to be jailed. A lot of reports have been made concerning people that have encountered accusations. The purpose was just to put them in trouble in order to make them spend away their money on fines for sexually abusing the under aged. Whereas, when actually verified was discovered not true.

❖

CHAPTER 6

Love of Prostitution

Sex in Exchange for Payment

It is a business or practice of engaging in sexual activity, in exchange for payment. It is a sexual service, which is rendered in order to make money. Therefore people engaging in this form of sexual activity for payment are called prostitutes.

A prostitute is known by some modes of dressing, which makes them almost naked or even completely naked. There are club prostitutes, who dance half or completely naked in clubs just to make sure more customers are coming in and as well as to make their own money besides their salaries. A prostitute can greet anyone so very closely — known and unknown persons — most especially if you are a man, quite differently.

Her supposed reason is you can possibly make an additional customer and if so, that is business booming. And that means more money also. She can hang around bars with pretension to buying something; whereas it is a medium to searching for customers. Her make-up, style and paces on the ground when walking are completely aimed towards her target.

Dressed to Seduce

All together making her advert. The aim is to draw the attention of men to herself and then make more customers. If you are then concerned, you must fall due to her positive expectation.

She can decide to put a phone on her ear without even talking to anybody for a distance along the way side; provided her strolling up and down is able to fetch her with something positive at the end of the day. The pretension of a phone call is a sort of umbrella to covering up the walk she is making. Imagine someone can put on a full gown trouser for outdoor without pant.

Is that not up to something? Even when she is healthy and okay and not that she does not have. Some are up to something; not all are usually genuine if you ask me. It is a call for something.

Inasmuch as clothes can define whoever puts them on, at a particular point in time, the concerned personalities will immediately turn costumers because they must approach you, which is your expectation in the first place while the mode of dressing. And what was she looking for in the first place? She is looking for money through this medium in order to be able to put food on her table and as well as to take care of other necessities.

What is the Primary cause of Prostitution?

The primary question is what causes prostitution? Allurement is number one. Mothers are very close to almost all their daughters. Some bad mothers have used this medium to speak a poisonous word into the minds of their daughters. Somebody, take care of the venom of a serpent as far as bad advice is concerned. Such words can come up in the form of sugar or honey, in that one would hardly know that it is a total disaster in the nearest future, if applied.

It is very very hard to turn down an advice, which humbly comes to you, with a manner of humility by the adviser meanwhile concealing up the disaster it carries— aiming at something in your life—the listener. It is hard to turn down even a betrayer of trust, who humbly comes to you for advice. It is hard to turn down a destroyer that humbly comes to you with sweat words, in order to create loopholes.

The Words of a Bad Mother

The word of a bad mother is a trigger, which pushes a gun to release either right or wrong bullets. Out of shame such a mother has the feelings to leave her husband, but can't due to matrimonial ties. But perhaps she thinks within herself that an alternative could be made by her daughter, to fill in the gap.

"My daughter are you happy in this poverty situation of ours? Please, remove us from it. You must do everything possible to blow debris off your parents eyes. Don't you see your mates? Jessica brought a bag of rice and some pieces of clothes for her mother in my presence the other day.

Instantly, as your mother, I was ashamed to identify with her and was immediately shy. In short, the glory of grief griped me like a cold." "Why mama?" "Because there's none to do the same for me. Can't you see? Who do I have except you." "Ah! Mama, it hasn't come to that."

"Look at my head, it has started to develop grey hair. And who knows tomorrow? We are tired of living in a mound house; besides. Please, birth us your parents in turn. If there is anything you can do to help us with this situation, even totally alleviate it. It is a total syndrome over us and I just can't take it anymore."

"Mama, I am sorry. It's just that I didn't know how you were feeling and how it is with you right now. But I want to further my education." "If you can help us to train your siblings, we your parents will be very much glad about that. My daughter, please, do us proud. Please, do us a favour."

Imagine all those who depend on that small thing between her legs. It is a pity, some ladies are finished on this basis. May God have mercy on some homes, where people do not think twice or juxtapose on their decision before action. Because of this many have jammed with ritualists who ended their lives. To God be the glory.

If you are the type who has no say for yourself, it is high time you got matured. Grow for good and for Christ's sake. Remember each life has accountability by the possessor, to the Sovereign Lord.

Sacrificing for your Family Members

How I wish there is a natural microscope for someone to be able to see everything from wherever he or she is. Lady, you are happily sacrificing for your family members (with your blood and not even your sweat this time around), as to say it's a normal thing that someone must provide for his or her family. If you now overdo all these systems by blood — performing blow jobs — to fulfil tasks imposed on you by your family members. You must know how a man feels with a woman when it comes to matrimony.

Your family members are another case entirely. They will rise up and say, "Our in-law is a stupid man; we don't know what he is doing with our daughter and sister."

A responsible woman says to the husband by action, "Respect my family and perform your obligations," even when he has. You are another lippy on your own. We do not question you of whatsoever you do with your body that the Lord God has given you. We are not trying to encroach on you with a kind of controversial interference; please, get me right. Cares emerge out of a sincere love or likeness.

Neither have we any audacity to restrict you of whatsoever usage you choose to make with your privates. It is your own. One thing is sure, which you must understand, if you are allowed with too much freedom and you end up having sex with many men during your single days, you may end up even becoming a prostitute, and there is every tendency that you may have problems with whomsoever you're going to meet as your future husband. That time, you are not a man and as such collective responsibility must set in whether you like it or not.

The simple fact is that all those men, (with different size organs), which you have mated with, might have beaten your spouse with a trillion percentage of satisfaction, as far as you are concerned. And so, don't you rather think it is hard for you to tolerate him. Every little mistake of him is going to be rated as a very big offence. Because you are lagging with the full joy to stay with him. And as a prostitute, you can't tell me that you've not sold part of your joy. You can imagine the irritation now right?

Be Quick to Unshackle Yourself

Lippi can precede lippy here and all men can't tolerate this, which we know. And don't you think that such a woman, without any respect for her man, (the one she calls her husband), is risking her marriage? Of course yes. The lesson is that, as too much of everything is bad, if you find yourself in this shackle, even before you pray to God for mercy and deliverance or rescue, rush and quickly look for away to come out of it. Heaven helps those who help themselves. If you consider the money in it, my sister you can never graduate out of it as a delivered. May the good God help your week-point in Jesus' name.

Be Careful of Wrong Advice

It may not necessarily have to be by food alone one can get any bewitchment. Word can as well do a similar work as poisonous food on the basis of witchcraft or bewitchment. In the case of the woman and her daughter, what has worked there? Is it not words? Be careful of the word, which carries with it wrong advice.

Jesus warned us against the bread of the Sadducees and the Pharisees (Mt 16:6). And such a questionable word could be an advice from anybody with full of doses. Whenever a divine advice is released this way, many at times look outside, mostly when we think we are too familiar with our homes and conclude that our homes have no problems.

Who betrayed Samson? The brethren of course. Similarly, who betrayed Jesus Christ the Messiah? Still the brethren of course. In a nutshell, know the kind of advice you accept and the one not to. As the devil is typically on a serious trail, looking for those whom to destroy or devour, he can use anybody around you mechanically and otherwise; provided he is able to achieve his aim. I therefore decree and declare that the devil's aim towards us to be unachievable in Jesus' name.

The outsiders you listen to, their advice also matters a lot. To avoid being victimised, you must be vigilant. Friends, like boyfriends and girlfriends could also stand out for Satan, on the basis of misleading someone into embarking on an undesirable business, which could if care is not taken ruin your entire life or even flop your real business.

When a friend says something with some backup examples, you no longer take time to find out whether or not it is true. All you do is jump and dabble into it, out of enthusiasm or fashion, without any considerable foundation. Why? And you are here blaming after all is said and done; when you were to take just a common decision by yourself.

May we never be rash in Jesus' name. Can we say it was anxiety? Owing to it not being checked, it has ended up birthing a castigation. Before we are to blame anybody else for being responsible for our misfortune, we must remember to beat back our minds, far back to memory lane and then sort out where we missed our steps, which landed us in an undesirable place.

Flattered beyond Self-Control

We are also liable to blame in most of our mistakes. It is always like that, with the case of human beings. Bad people teach you a lesson to be wise, while of course the good people teach us examples of the good roads to take in life. When anxiety would have been controlled by you without any mistake. Beat your mind back to those days.

Remember when you were over-flattered and thrilled even beyond self control. And at the end of the day, you got no human option to actually put it under control, other than to apply the advice. Look at where it landed you? King Darius did against brother Daniel in (Dn 6:1-9).

Hi Angela, after you gave birth to your first child when your old friend visited you from the States, what happened?

You looked at yourself with much ego and a haughty look and actively awakened. Suddenly you broke out saying: "I'm angry to stay with this useless man and spend the rest of my lifespan with him; never no never."

Inexplicable Mistake

Your so called husband instantaneously became a non-entity in your mind. Imagine that kind of inexplicable mistake of yours! "I must move," you concluded. "Can't you see? Look at me, the difference is cleared. Do we need any prophet to differentiate us? Someone show me the way now or else I die here."

Were those words not your statements? "I am dying here," you added. When that one filled you with every one of your required info, you dumped your baby on that subsequent night and eloped for her side and that was the end of your marriage.

You said you were too beautiful to stay with one man. You said your private is too big for him alone. You said how can a gorgeous lady of your calibre do squats with a good for nothing man like your husband.

Are you blaming me that your child is a slave to the present wife to your formal husband and her children? It was your plan and decision in the first place. I do believe you are enduring the benefit of a wrong action you took right now.

You said you are too far behind your equals for that reason you must do anything humanly possible to change the situation around you. Can you eat your cake and have it?

If at all, it is not in everything. Where is your so called human attraction that you once felt? You have sold all of them.

Where is your Beauty?

Where is your beauty? You have sold that as well. Even all your buttock has gone inside, why? What did you do to merit all this? Oh what a shame! A car who wanted to run speed, in order to arrive at its destination even earlier than expected, here it is parked by the roadside, why? Can you see the whole lot of traffic jamb you caused to yourself?

Oral discussion, which is related to obscenity is a trigger, which can easily birth such action. Run from it. The truth of the matter is that, the mind of the listener is already overwhelmed with the talk. The only solution is God's divine intervention. "The death of a dog is usually caused by the inability to snuff or sniff."

The next stage involves access to gadgets; you shouldn't open the website when you can't control your emotions. You begin to watch pornography just to get the full idea of what it's all about, but now you're inside with the inability to turn back.

Some inherited it from a parent or both parents. In DNA, there is every tendency that a child (out of all the children) must carry the characteristics and traits of the parents, whether good or bad; believe it or not. And so, if those parents happen to initiate that child in the category of the same act, it will be very hard for that child not to turn out a prostitute in her entire life because it must manifest.

Unchecked frustration from a broken heart in a relationship can also lead to it, as an unforeseen circumstance. It can lead to drinking and even smoking cigarettes or marijuana and cocaine, if care is not taken.

Demons have successfully influenced a majority of single ladies with the mind-set of getting themselves rich through using their private parts. For example with the insertion of certain substances in the privates, in order to be smuggled across borders to evade law enforcement, which is very easy for certain types of business personalities.

One Stone Two Birds

On arrival, she can be forced or officially be asked for sex, along with the substance to deliver. And if accepted, many have as a sport mated with five to seven men as a payment; in addition to the bargained business in the first place. It is a whole lot of money. Believe you me, as a lady likes using one stone to kill two birds, it will never end there. Many, through this method, have acquired prostitution.

Today, it is unavoidable due to the benefit it yields for them. It has made them even forget that there exists other alternatives for making their lives better, without illegal activities that one cannot defend (or maintain one's reputation), besides the threat of the law and the risk of imprisonment. And some will boldly say, "Who cares about reputation anymore?" As time waits for nobody, they resign themselves to going in any direction; provided they achieve their aim.

Back to the crux, in Genesis, human life was not actually bought and as such, people can choose what they do with their own, without the fear of being questioned to order. Life is too short, which everyone knows. But because our lives are concerned with one another, due to how we all are networked naturally, we are tied by the bond of brotherhood.

That is why it looks as if we engage in a kind of controversial action towards one another, due to collective responsibility. I believe this quickly reflects one's mind back to the garden of Eden. "Seeing without saying, can kill an adult. While being disobedient to a simple instruction, can kill a child."

Remember someone Cares about You

If you are under the influence of a controlling spirit and doing these questionable actions, don't forget that someone cares about you. Otherwise who cares if you die as a result of your mistakes? When you are offended or life generally treated you badly, try to encourage yourself and then find away out, which is a solution to your problem.

Get along with your life peacefully. If you scratch yourself based on the length of your fingernails, you might just get a cut that could bleed. Take life easy, for all hope is not lost. Competition or no competition, life is simply life itself. Life is only dangerous in the sense that it has no duplicate and when lost, that is the end.

There is nothing that isn't useful. For example, someone could be missing or reported missing by kidnappers and if reported that he or she is still alive, it will only take an intelligent prostitute to storm in the area and sleep with the men, even drug them if possible, and free the victim in question.

It has happened in some localities in the past, which I do believe is still applicable to date, that if you had no money for a ransom, you could use what you had to get what you actually wanted. In those days, (when it was not this devilish all over the globe), besides the sex as a kind of camouflage, there could be some diabolical powers and charms, which were added in order to enable the mission to be successfully accomplished.

She will never Accept You

Any lady who is deeply rooted in the act of prostitution, can hardly believe in matrimony. If you are a working class man and you aren't a high earner, you can approach her for marriage but she will never accept you. She will underrate you and conclude that you cannot take care of her. Most especially when she ruminates over her income, past or present, you are finished. You are better looking for some other ladies to approach, who are more likely to accept you. Not this first class lady; according to herself.

First class, must marry a man that she can answer to. I am not against any act of selection, in other words, I don't dispute the act of choices. "A cook must carefully select his or her cooking ingredients." Choice is undisputed, but we must avoid exaggeration.

At a time you can't tell me that you don't sometimes feel the usefulness of a husband in your life at your closet? Tell me, who is then ready now to spend the rest of his entire lifespan with a second class nigger like you? Forget about the face, which must always shine due to a constant make-up.

You can't Marry Yourself

Let me eulogise, if a complete beautiful pineapple should lose its juice, even though the peel might still be shining, who cares about the peel when the content has been carefully removed and is no more. Men do not eat glory in a thing like that. To say the truth, you cannot marry yourself, even if you are both the man and woman in your life. Men have seen groundnut-oil that they will never tell you they have seen. It is totally unspeakable.

Compare the pineapple with a door in the village with bad hinges, which a goat can still open even when locked, due to being over-used and its slackness. Don't you rather think it takes the complete grace of God for a miracle to take place here? Of course yes. Let's be sincere here to some degree.

The issue about prostitution cannot be over emphasised. If you jump from church to church in search of a miracle, (whereby God is omnipresent and omniscient), you are a prostitute. Change and turn to a new life. God blesses you.

❖

CHAPTER 7

Love of Dirty Jobs

Blue Films

This is the kind of undertaking, which most of the responsible governments and nations do not recognise and accept exists, by law. It could be existing secretly (in black form). It is a true saying that one man's poison is another man's meat. In some nations, this contributes as part of their resources. One would begin to wonder how could a nation be built on resources actually extracted from blue-films? All they do is to register the concerned people and get tax from them.

Some young ladies are very lazy; they believe in so much money and fun and so get themselves trapped in the act and render our society ruined with it. It also affects the local and national economy of wherever such is allowed to be practised legally or illegally without being checked both directly or indirectly.

Jezebel's fornication alone wrecked the economy of the entire nation of Israel (2 Kgs 9:22). That provoked Jehu's to carry out the purpose of his anointing, which was the mission to kill Jezebel, the daughter of king Ethbaal, ruler of the coastal Phoenician cities (now in Lebanon). Mind you, her children are all over this entire world until tomorrow. Many of them are those who mate with their same-bloods; rapists, killers, ritualists, fornicators, the cheats and many more.

Engaging in Naughty Business

Some ladies do engage in dancing naked as their profession. Can you imagine? All these are for the sake of money. And where are we going? The same thing pushed evil foolish men into bisexual acts as their profession for money (a common legalised currency by federal government), someone is engaging in a naughty business, in order to be able to survive by it. What a shame!

It is a true saying that, "the activities of man can create endless history." A little wonder why all this? Well, the truth is not far fetched, in the sense that every activity starts or commences from both the physical and spiritual realms, it is therefore a known fact that this was the choice they made beforehand.

Curses can even make a responsible fellow embark on dirty jobs such as blue-films. As far as nobody is useless, some people have become over lazy to the extent they have allowed themselves to be inclined with the devil, to switch them into doing evil.

The operators or actors might feel it is less strenuous as the first motive of every venture, is money motive. And after all, the reward for labour is salary. Therefore, if this can give them money, they will gladly appreciate. Not all sources of money are beneficial. Cash or money does not voice where it was made, neither does it tell where it goes.

Many undertakers of this bloody business, do not usually last. As everything is strength, even when they sometimes use power-up (drugs) there is nothing like natural, which is well used. On the contrary, if one rather misused his or her physical strength, there is no doubt if the result will be negative.

Natural power has a limit, one can use it excessively. But at the level of extremism, it can fail due to the law of diminishing return in nature. Excessive fun and pleasure, can be deadly at times. Too much of everything is completely bad.

❖

CHAPTER 8

Love of Illegal Business

Technology is Advancing

As the globe is getting broadened every now and then, technology is advancing also. Eventually, everybody wants to get it all. It is very unfortunate that not every nation has optimum standards of economy. Due to this, rural to urban migration and emigration is the order of the day because of the search for a greener pasture. Basically, rural to urban drift has been, it is and it will ever be.

The youths of nowadays have the belief that money answers all things, therefore they hunt for it at all costs; this their motive. Even if it means engaging in all kinds of illegal business, provided they get their requisites in due time. They want speedy cash.

Some have money because of their involvement in the act of selling hard drugs—cocaine. This is a thing all federal governments in every nation reject or abolish by law. So many people are just into it as though it is a legal business. They neither work nor engage in any other genuine business to contribute their quota to the progress of the nation of wheresoever they recite.

Money Doublers

Secondly, money doublers attract the interest of youths — very highly—in order to generate their resources. Ask me, if those who double money, have money, what is the essence of deciding to double for people by asking you to bring certain amounts of money to double for you? He or she would not even let you know that he has that kind of money. 419 is a game, which can lead the doer into jail any time or day that he or she is caught.

So many people womanise in order to get sum for fun and pleasure. Use what you have, to get what you want is from this perspective. Believe it or not, whatever you get from the wrong source, is a complete exchange with something else from you. For some of them, it is not 100% their fault. Evil spirits can possess them in order to lure them into it (while they themselves could choose it). It gives them money.

Some ladies who are possessed by evil spirits, can be sent specifically as delegates to go and pay a concerned fellow with a certain amount of money, in order to make him rich. This is where the dragging of women comes from, not because of beauty, height, race, back-ground, education, socialisation etc., as some ignorant people think.

Discover what makes you their Hot Cake?

Aren't you sometimes surprised by those who have fought to get a lady, yet still leave her single in the end? This is after he has succeeded in emptying the contents of the vessel. May the good God help us. If you are a hot cake to some people—find out why—else you become a victim, if not checked. And if care is not taken, you might have lost something very important before you realised it. Basically, if you have nothing to offer, no one wants you. And so, I leave you with the issue to juxtapose yourself.

Some elements have assassin and criminal records as their profession. Some do private surveillance jobs, in order to monitor people for those concerned, yet find it difficult to achieve by themselves. With the right help, it's a done deal. They are like radios, who gather and disseminate information, for a price. Money is indeed the root of all evil.

Lusting for money pushes people to embark on every negative process, in order to secure it at all costs. Illegal business could be anything one does, which earns them an income and which is totally against societal conformity, even before God and the government.

CHAPTER 9

Love by Force

Rape

There is no enjoyment in whatever you archive by force. Ladies and gentle men, the joy one gets from such, is a complete afternoon shadow of glory of which man does not even know what glory is all about; only God can tell what it is to Him. Whether it is food or not, you don't know and you can't tell. It lasts like intimidation and finally fades away. And there is no fast rule about this truth. It is plain.

Some group feel that if you toast or talk to a single lady or girl and she turns down your proposal, you can use force to be accepted by her. Even if you could be accepted as a result of much pressure on her, remember your seed of love cannot germinate in her stony heart by force. If you take what does not belong to you, something must leave you. This is one of the secret laws of nature. Jack Dawson died in the Titanic because he met Rose, a supposed wife to another man.

The fact that you are dejected being looked down upon doesn't mean you must react that way. The fact that you are humiliated doesn't mean the end of the world for you. There are alternatives who are even egger to date your kind of person. Lack of access to the real target is what seems to be the problem here. Any love which does not come from the minds of both sexes, can never work and it is usually not enjoyable. Can two work together, except they are of the same spirit (Am 3:3). Thus, if she says no, please, do not force her unless you want trouble.

What is done in Secret

Rape, you know how much the law against it is so very high with punishment in the cult of law by the chief judge through law enforcement agents. I suggest one must abstain from what will land one in trouble. It is totally shameful to explain what is done in secret that is against the law (Eph 5:1).

They will ignorantly rate the girl, perhaps because they can beat her physically and there will be no revenge due to her family background. And so, embark on a forceful kind of rape to satisfy their urge. When there is no one to avenge the innocent, the Lord God will (Ps 94:1). When critically analysed this act of sexual abuse, one will find that the motive behind this is a boy—who doesn't love the girl involved—but has an uncontrollable desire to discharge his semen (at all costs).

Therefore, as the law is against rape, this can land him in jail if care is not taken. There are some reasons when you go jail, you will still feel normal but not with the case of a rape. It is a shameful thing, which nobody likes to identify with.

Except the Lord Intervenes

I bet you, the stigma will ever be there. No matter the effort put in place by the rapist to actually erase the record, it will ever be there. Except the Lord God intervene there is no remedy. Some people develop love on someone because of his or her performance, which is either sex in bed (in profession or in knowledge), with that alone they are satisfied.

A girl could be dating more than one guy at a time. In most cases, the one that is directly in her mind, may not be the one who satisfies her in bed. And so, she can decide to fall completely in love even though he is a wrong man, due to his action in bed. Groups of girls are usually interested in guys who are very intelligent in school.

Without even being toasted, they are already in love because of their academic aspirations, as a benefit from him. And that makes many of them to begin to friend whom they weren't supposed to. By forced love in this case, it can make you even commerce a family of your own earlier than usual.

I have seen many guys who could not go far in their academic pursuit because of this. Many are in the villages due to wrong relationships, kept somehow in the past during school days. Do you know what that means? An education or career is forfeited. Girls or ladies of nowadays jump into relationships by force because of target benefits, such as material and financial wealth. So, any bad fellow (who is a womaniser) easily gets advantage over them, due to the fact that they are going to flock him with more than expected; he can serve them by stretching his hand to entice them.

What a Mistake!

If care is not actually taken, forced love can make you fall into an unwanted home or family. What a mistake! Don't let finance, beauty or anything, lead you into being deceived into embarking or eloping and cleaving to a man you don't know so well.

Being betrothed is outdated nowadays. If you don't know what is good for you, or you are the type that has no choice, you can still suffer. Someone can be a victim of bewitchment—with a love potion—such that he or she no longer has a choice. Lacking some sort of personal policy, (I can call it a syndrome), makes some people suffer unnecessarily. If you know what is good for you, I suggest you go for it, rather than just succumbing to whatever comes your way.

Evil societal personalities have captured so many people by force in order to initiate them into their kind of ways. This they do in order to increase the population of those that belong to their group.

In universities, if you are under siege or targeted and you are a guy that likes women so much, they can use girls to set you up in order to lure you into their group. Failure to do so or comply, results in either a huge sum of money being paid or you no longer go to that school; unless you did not fall into their trap.

Belief in Effizy

If you take by force what doesn't belong to you, it is either you die or you lose. The mysteries of the world are far more than just common understanding by a layman. Most single ladies or girls believe so much in love from above like from across the seashore. I mean, the local guys even if they are single with a career, with so much love to unleash on them, they just don't care nor even want to be considerate at all. What they believe is effizy, in order to intimidate their equals: fellow girls or ladies.

Really, such can draw the attention of others to them. A girl or a lady could be very good to her fellow lady or girl in the act of sheepishly; you can't tell. A single girl or a single lady can fall in love with a prince simply because she is having the intention that as the first son of the royal king, definitely, he must be the future king as an apparel to the throne and that automatically means she becomes the future queen of the royal kingdom.

People can fall in love by force. Love for an position in the nearest future can be so very rigid by them at times. In that case, you see already proposals in courtship suddenly parted due to a superior that just jumped in their midst.

Strategic Methods

They can for example find away to introduce application of a system like autocratic power through speech by advising as an adviser with strategic evil methods in order to have the girl that's all. Some guys can level allegations against the fiancée: the girl in question. By laying a hand on any girl, for her hand in marriage, as an opportunity to push the old one away by action. In the real sense, that must be confiscation.

If I may ask, where was the new one when the old one started? If not because girls can change overnight with just a common word; in that the rightful owner will no longer have a saying, someone would defend her to the core. The fake can proudly declare that the poor underrated family of the girl must never reject the offer of the prince. The prince can have anything he wants in the land. What must be, must be. You don't force love. Do you?

A true love has no regard for colour, race, social class, background, title, education, rather it maintains its simple nature. In other words, it is simply natural. Therefore at this junction, the will of God is never the will of man, in some cases (Is 55:8).

❖❖

CHAPTER 10

Love of Animals & Pets

The Love of Animals

Actually, nature is much more than just beauty and elegance. The aged animal is being revealed by history older than man on earth. However, we bless God for whom He is. Everybody likes animals. Due to this fact that certain elements like animals, it has led to keeping pets domestically.

Birds per se are beautiful. It is being observed among the popular Westerners that most of the aged people who hate loneliness resign to keeping birds in their homes. They do this in order to keep their home lively and noisy. The fact is that it is very difficult for some of them to find any of their grandchildren who would like to stay with them; probably due to the condition of living.

It yields income to the owner when it gives birth. Actually, it interests you to see a bird when it is feeding its offspring. They are mostly the animals that enjoy the highest atmosphere. When you take a look at the sky during the day, maybe after it has rained or under a heavy sun, you can see how eagles hover on it.

Cats are very soft and gentle animals. It always keeps the owner with some company. It is the type of animal that mostly prefers staying indoors and feeding from plates. Even if it goes out to roam, with other cats, it returns home to eat and feel the owner's body, by carefully moving around him or her to rub its body on theirs.

Medical Treatment for Animals

The only disadvantage is that any clothes the owner wears, will always fill with its hair. Cats also carry lice or ticks, which suck its blood and cause skin disease. This means further expense for the owners. It must be treated with vaccines and the house must be well ventilated in order to avoid it.

If otherwise occurs beyond normal control by vaccines, I advice that one consults a veterinary doctor. Glory be to God that in the Western world, every animal has a doctor. And so, whenever the need arises, the owner immediately takes it there for a treatment.

In addition, some untrained cats can be bad. For example, they can feed on food and then defecate on it; mostly Gari. This is African staple food, which probably must belong to its owner. They can also steal meat and fish from their owners, as well as the public; except in a situation whereby they are well trained.

One of the economic values of having a cat is that it can hunt game and kill and bring it to their owner or hide and eat it later (or vomit it up in order to feed its offspring etc). A female cat can yield income to the owner when it gives birth. Some bad people can train cats for sex.

The Advantage of Training Animals

Dogs are one of the animal species that possess half of the human senses. Dogs to be candid, are very intelligent. Hunters keep dogs for both securities and for the hunting of game and the killing of other animals for meat; either for sale or personal consumption. Dogs can even hunt game by itself, either for its owner, itself or its puppies.

Some people purposely keep dogs for pets. They also train them in case of emergency in order to help alert them or even alert neighbours for help when the need arises. In the Western world, rape is very common. Due to this women usually stroll with dogs, for protective measures, even before anybody renders them with any assistance. Apart from that, generally dogs are kept for security against intruders, criminals and such.

Police can purposely train certain dogs for special duties, like to trace the legs of an immediately escaping criminal. Some dogs are specifically trained against hard drugs—cocaine. These sets of dogs do expose drug addicts to the police. Even if the fellow hide it in his or her body, the dog will keep backing until the person in question is taken to the hospital for verification.

Dogs are also used in producing films. They are also used for dog sports competitions, which can yield the owner with some income. Dogs can also swim, which can serve as a rescue for other animals. You can easily find examples with some animal regarding house boundaries. Go to the nomads and you will see the work of dogs; how they are used in monitoring various types of cattle such as bulls, sheep and cows etc.

The Lewd use of Animals

Dogs can also be used by those that produce blue-films. Owing to its fast ability to learn, they can also be trained how to mate with humans, whether male or female. For this reason, some lonely sexually abused ladies keep dogs as pets merely to have sex with them. They make sure the dogs in their houses are well trained in order to intelligently know how to mate with them. When they are done and the dogs now know how, they no longer bother about having men around them.

Even horses; many people keep and rear them not merely for transportation but because it's powerful, some people see that it must be very good in sex also, so that they such can be satisfied to the maximum level of their requirements. Plus, it can serve a very long time for that purpose. May God have mercy on some elements who indulge in such acts.

Another observation about this particular animal by some humans is that it serves to them as meat. Some dirty film producers also use it to produce with other fellow horses and with humans. Worst of all, these concerned ladies are usually happy to produce such films for money, which even the whole world can watch. Surprisingly, any blue-film produced with horses involved (whether horse with horse or horse with human), is very expensive and it sells even more than other dirty films.

Sexually Transmitted Diseases

The truth is that people will be curious about how animals like horses can be trained to develop sexual interest in humans and still be able to perform. The organ of a male horse is very big and long. And due to that, some useless ladies in this category will want to try it because they just want to try something new. According to some of them, it is indeed satisfactory. But little did they know that anything that has advantage also has disadvantage. Some therefore get HIV/AIDS, syphilis and some other related diseases from this source.

In the Western world, there are some public animals such as birds, doves, pigeons, rabbits and grass-cutters, ducks and others, which you can normally find in small streams that flows across the middle of cities. They bathe and drink water from it. So many people purposely come there to feed them with all kinds of foods.

Fine. But, on the contrary, some of them do feed them because those are the species that all belong to the spiritual realm. Indirectly, it can also mean feeding their neighbours as far the specie is concerned.

The Love of Pets

Pets are animals kept domestically merely for fun and pleasure. They help to keep the home of whoever keeps them lively and busy. They also make their owners feel free, as though they were living with a companion (even though there's a difference between humans and ordinary animals).

Like dogs, cats are very popular mainly because they are meek, soft, cool, and quiet. An angry cat can beat a dog even if it is big or small. It arouses the owner with certain alerts if need be most especially, on an emergency.

The Disadvantages of having Pets

The disadvantage of keeping pets is that they can be very high maintenance. When the occasion calls for taking a dog out for a stroll, you simply must, without hesitation. Also feeding and bathing them regularly. Plus they must have their own houses or cages, unless you leave the dog and cat freely within your compound. In that case, it must be well trained not to bite people; except criminals who intend to steal, harass or rape.

In addition, you must be tolerant, as your home will always be filthy, especially with their constant shedding. So, you must be ready to clean every now and then and all this will cost you with much expenses.

So many people keep dogs and cats for other purposes like good and bad messages against innocent people in the world. They can errand them to go and attack people in order to accomplish their mission. Besides that, they also serve by mating them in their houses like human beings. If you talk to any single lady and she says no and you want to force her to accept you, the dog may react. Mostly if the dog is in a relationship with her, the reaction might even be worse.

❖

CHAPTER 11

Love of Beauty

Viewed as Attractive

Humanly, beauty starts first from the face. Usually, when the face is cleaned without pimples, it is attractive and eased make-up. A good looking young lady and a very handsome young man are good in promoting any fashion. When they dress, it actually makes them look good and nice in their outfit.

We have black-beauty. These are found among the black race; except those bought as slaves in the various concerned countries in the Western part of the world including America. As they would say "fine sexy without pimples". Their black-skins shine as if naturally oiled. The yellow people and the chocolates are found among the black race also.

We also have the white race that have the white skin; mostly the Ukraine. It is still the same thing as the black we just discussed. There are also the red people who are mostly found among the white race also; the Albanians. These sets of humans are naturally red in complexion.

We have also the Caucasian; even the the albino that can be found on both races are also included. They are plainly known among the black-race as albinos while in the midst of the white-race, they are notified by their eyes-balls. So far so good, I do believe that we've treated the six colours of human beings.

Having thoroughly viewed the beauty of the world, you find now that there is no lady that is not beautiful. How? Because it all depends on her level of self maintenance. When a humanly considered young ugly lady is well nourished and catered for and with quality cosmetics, believe you me her true colour will radiate immediately.

True Beauty is Never Bought

Naturally, when you take a close look at every lady, there must be a part of her body that one will credit her with confirmation that she is cute or fine here. Due to the criticisms and distinctions against ugly and beauty, which some human beings do make or exhibit, some ladies resign to bleaching their skins in order to appear among beauties in the eyes of the concerned public personalities. Little did they know that they are incurring much disadvantages on themselves.

One of the highest problems a person can cause to themselves is to use money to buy sickness or even death in the future. When you take a look at the same particular ladies, they look older than their ages. And if peradventure they have any ailment, which necessitates surgery even before curing, they are just finished and they may likely not survive it.

Beauty is never bought as some people thought. Instead, they are messing up the whole thing. It is simply natural. Please, only maintain it and have your true skin radiate its true colour.

Discriminations

Some ladies do exercise discrimination and racism on others they humanly find less beautiful than they are. This leads to making distinctions among themselves; whereby nobody created themselves. You are just lucky to be whom you are naturally. And so, give God a praise that made of you rather than castigating and looking down on others with less value to your standard.

Drop your claim of self superiority and pride of nature or better still put it under control in order to be able to relate with people around you for good. If your fellow human is too slim for your liking, it shouldn't be an ill-business to you as a person. It was never the complete fault of any pauper who found it so very difficult at the earlier stage to maintain his/her skin before getting to a certain level where it looks relatively dull.

Regular Maintenance

Nature requires maintenance, as well as the artificial. Therefore, if you have the opportunity to have water for a bath twice or thrice daily, don't conclude by saying everybody is just as lucky as you. All fingers are not equal. Everything requires regular maintenance.

Feeding has so much to do with beauty also. Don't you think eating thrice daily even twice are hard to some people let alone? Of course. Some have even converted their hunger into a forced state of fasting and prayers (just to fill in the gap).

To everything there is a level and extremism induces people with the law of diminishing return. Too much of everything is bad. It is a complete fool who laughs at another fellows poor standard. Quote me here: anyone that can laugh at you is not to be taken for a friend. In short, he or she is an enemy, trust me. Many have wasted away, due to an inability to take good care of themselves.

Disregarding God's Unique Creations

So, someone is beautiful. Disregarding God's creations is equivalent as disregarding the Lord Himself, who made them. It is not compulsory that you must like everybody but don't laugh at them or abuse them. Stay away from them if you can't condone them or are uncomfortable with their presence.

Every human being is distinctively created by God for a purpose, which you can't know about, no matter how hard you may experiment to confirm and conclude. There must be one or two things yet to be ascertained on a body of an individual. Whether you like it or not, that is the truth of the matter. Each person is a unique fellow, find out.

❖

CHAPTER 12

Love of Handsome

Preferring Quality Ingredients

Categorically, many people select guys that are very handsome, either for casual friendship or for a relationship (above all for marriage). It is very good anyway. These sets of ladies in particular have reasons for this; equivalent to a good cook who prefers quality ingredients for making a delicious meal. In the second world of human beings, a handsome or beautiful person is a hot cake for demonic activities. That is where the idea of bleaching mostly comes from, in order to blend with the required level of beauty for a favour.

Handsome per se is not a big deal. It is a thing of nature. And that doesn't mean who is not too handsome has no advantage in life. And nobody should deny his or her fellow human beings of their human reckon with or even a regard. No one is a lord over the other, unless God makes them one of the messiahs He uses, as a tool to discharge His miracles, no one can forcefully lord over others.

There is a level of handsome a person can be endowed by the Sovereign Lord. I would advise that any class Jehovah levelled you up with, you should appreciate; be glad and be proud to thank God for making you. It is a known fact that there's no born of element which doesn't like good thing. But it shouldn't become a thing of worship or lust, to discriminate others with.

To everything that has advantage, there is also an opposite disadvantage. So, many guys have love that could be so very dangerous in the sense that not all which glitters is gold. For example, externally the body can be delightful, while the inner man can be a complete devil incarnate.

The Problem with being Over Selective

A handsome husband is a thing of joy for a woman. But in case, a less than very handsome one according to human distinction comes your way provided he is original, don't hesitate to embrace and then find out from God whether you are meant for each other. Over selecting is a very big future problem to those that have practiced it. Human guarantee without God does not yield any expected result.

Some believe that a handsome husband automatically means handsome children. They got it very wrong in the sense, a humanly regarded ugly person can give birth to the most epitome if you don't know. God is the maker of quality babies (Ps 127:3).

So many people that are fond of making distinctions prefer using handsome and beautiful elements to grace their occasions. Due to this advantage, (that handsome guys have), it induces them the advantage of having as many women as possible. Even the lustful ladies who are so desperate about men, do spend some money in order to have them for their usual enjoyment, at their quiet moment even for fun. Even some fake and figurehead married women have forfeited their marriages for handsome afternoon men. Due to jealousy, some fake guys who underrate themselves, do bleach up their skins in order to suit the class or system.

Abusing God's Handiwork

Ignorantly, they forgot that artificial and natural are too different things altogether. Handsomeness has grades or levels. This is noted by carefully taking a closer look at the skin and face of any guy. Elegant men appear elegantly. And that doesn't mean that a less than elegant person (according to your standard), should be automatically ridiculed to scorn. Avoid it, else, God may fight you for abusing His handiwork.

God that varies the level of handsomeness is not a fool. Since He created human beings, He knows us better than we know ourselves. He knew beforehand that too much beauty/handsomeness can be problematic at times. And so, He gives you according to your destiny.

Some are afflicted with sickness, skin diseases, poisoned half-to-death, accused, raped, even killed because of beauty/

handsomeness. And so, the percentage you are endowed could be as a result of your protective measure. More than that could land you in trouble; God actually knows better. Therefore, it is for your own good that you emerge with your own possessed level of beauty/handsome, so don't be jealous of your neighbour or in any way regret your standard.

❖

CHAPTER 13

Lustful Love

Merely Focused on the Sex Act

Love is humanly considered lustful when those who practice it on the other, are not really serious about it. When a love is merely focused on the bed action, it can be called a lustful love. In which case, the moment they get the particular targeted aim from the opposite sex, he/she dashes into thin air. And that is the end of that.

In most cases, the treatment you receive from these sets of people when you run across them, is irritable and thought provoking; because they are wrong contacts irrespective of their status: whether married or not.

In the sexual circle, whoever has this partial likeness that we all call love, does not usually respect honesty when it comes to moral issues. He or she just can't control it. Even when married — if God doesn't intervene — they're bound to commit adultery.

Love is Cheap when it Lacks Morality

"No wonder I do not doubt who is living in an up-stair can still eat sand." Such a person is desperate to sleep around with any fellow, when opportunity comes their way. These sets of people are egger to spend their money for the opposite sex, just to catch some fun. But when it comes to having some responsibility, they run! In fact any lustful love doesn't last. It was gotten so very cheaply, so it gets lost just as easily.

This is the reason why you see some elements lured into deviating from their responsibilities; to family, work and the rest. A situation where someone suddenly becomes an infidel; you understand that kind thing. Infidelity is a curse, a curse in the sense that the strange lover they met, must work on them for his advantage. Imagine a spouse who left home for work, only to end up with a late night. Meanwhile, the other spouse is busying praying for the successful day and their return.

Nay, it's an abomination instead, that the wayward spouse is dancing on another persons body, as though they'd never been married. Many salaries have been lost to this, as a result of striving to wet the ground, in order to avoid escalation about their secret indulgence.

The question is, why at all a double life? Who initiated it first? How is it going to end? What is the mind of God towards it? You are neither the first nor even the last that is going to ask these questions about nature (why life treats him or her the way it does) till Christ returns, believe you me. What you see and experience daily, poses you with a lot of questions yet to be answered.

God must Release Revelation

These, I strongly believe, have been a sort of burden in the mind of many. And I'm so very sure are still rigmaroled up and down in the minds of the concerned, in search for answers. Except God releases a revelation, you can never know why and how, or even what.

I am talking to you dear reader, try to avoid depression concerning the issues of life, which are so humanly complicated. Fundamentally, situations have forced us to accept certain issues, as though they are part of our cultures. There are many human activities, which have been forcefully introduced into systems that didn't formally or culturally exist, yet have now been broadly accepted, because we had no other choice.

And many need to ask questions, but the fact is they have not really found a real contact who has had the experience to be able to answer such personal questions. If you must not suffer too much, you need to learn by example. Sometimes when you are taught by an experienced person, you maybe reluctant to take that as the truth. Simply because the revelation did not come directly from you and moreover, you lack a concrete evidence to stamp the answers to be the original truth.

Many of us are into this dilemma as a syndrome. And except God helps you, you just can't really paddle to sail through or across the Red Sea, concerning issues of life successfully. For example, in the book of Genesis 2:7, it was the image that actually came first before the Spirit.

Many are know-it-alls, whose words are never taken to be anything. Even many suggestions have been rejected for real. Might it be that it did not come from an expected source or from a personality you respected with high esteem. *"A man is equal to his word."* If you are not welcome, neither can your words be. It is not really your fault nor the fault of the teacher in question or your acquaintance. You know why, not everything can work for everybody.

The Grace of God Speaks for Us

Here is where the grace of God speaks for humans, invariably. You can imagine where the grace of God will cover up for one, to operate in doing anything the other cannot, just to go free without being punished even with just a mere attempt to do it. The grace works specifically along with everyones covenant with God. And no one can really tell everything about him or herself with the Sovereign Lord.

Naturally, the Lord God only allotted a proportion, as our human concern appropriates, to know about the hidden agenda of His creations. And so, humanly, we all do not know everything. If God does not reveal something, you just can't know it. And so, the extent you know about whom you are in God will actually determine the limit your humanity can go or rather permit you to operate with success by God.

You will be afraid because you don't know what to do. Just as birds don't fly as broad as the sky, but on a routine basis, so we all have a line of our ministries. It is actually true that each must run across as many as necessarily possible, at a particular point in time, but not possibly all, because nature decides on that.

God will not Sponsor your Wrong Choices

As a result, many have dabbled into wrong businesses and ended up with failure. If you make a wrong choice, the grace of God may not sponsor you to the infinity with success. And anything you stopped halfway in no doubt did not succeed. Marriages have failed. Educations have failed. Reproductions have failed. Businesses have failed. The buying of assets such as land, houses, cars on higher purchase, companies, schools, shops, etc., have all failed as a result of this.

Many have actually made a lot of promises who could not meet up with their promises, because the Lord God hadn't sanction it, and as a result such individuals couldn't really succeed. Otherwise, who will sponsor it? Friendships have failed because you can't just be friends with everybody; no, it's not possible. Whoever is everyones friend is an enemy of God, according to James 4:4. Not everyone even likes God, let alone you, a common person in our society.

In addition, embarked careers have failed because of imitations, which were never part of their respective destinies. Then take a full look at how you dress, I guess you do have a mirror. Does it really fit you? Or probably you got it by imitation just to blend with the reigning fashion. Must everybody do the same thing! Just because you have the money to buy something, doesn't mean you must actually buy everything, no, never.

Cease doing the Forbidden

There are places we all must not go. There are foods we all must not eat. There are styles of clothes that we all must never sow. There are dances, which we all must never dance. Each life has a purpose to give God a praise. In your layman's simple knowledge, you must grasp what I am trying to marshal out here.

The truth of the matter, which I'm unveiling to you is this; whatever you do that doesn't give God a praise in your life, don't continue to do it and never repeat it again, if you have tried it before and it didn't work out, because it is not a part of your covenant with God. He blesses you. Even if you force your grace to go there, at the long run you must fail, no doubt.

The double life in question, started from the Garden of Eden. No one actually came into being all by him or herself. God created only two people (Adam and Eve) directly. After which every other person came as a result of God's spoken word, saying thus: "Be fruitful, and multiply, and replenish the earth..." (Gn 1:28 KJV)

Today, it is only God Himself that can tell how His word is doing a scientific work on the semen of a man in the womb of a woman, in order to bring about a foetus that forms a human being. It is indeed a complete mystery in the reproduction cycle, in the sense it is silenced to the understanding of mankind. Wow! Amazing!

However, before the forbidden fruit was eaten, the mind of humanity was one, (with only positive thoughts); one decision, one action and one reaction. So let's take a critical look at the forbidden fruit.

The Two Faces of Forbidden Fruit

The contents of which were defined by the Sovereign Lord, as double (Gn 2:7); one part being negative and the other positive. For example, negative fruit involves the knowledge of evil, calamity and punishment. Which includes things like: sickness, pain, poverty, failure, disappointment, disgrace, rising and falling, humiliation, delay, slow motion, barrenness, miscarriage, sick government, sick nations, corruption, stealing, murder, killing, ritualism, serving of juju/images (totally abhorred by God), evil jealousy, adultery, fornication, lies, betrayal, confiscation, land disputes, abominations, anal sex, oral sex, carnal sex, homosexuality, heterosexuality, incest (between parents and their own children), trickery, deceit, joblessness, flop, felony, charms, magic and all kinds of atrocities, witches and wizards, occultism, evil powers, agents of the devil, vampire, assassin, evil darkness, egotism, gloom, evil recruits and many more such examples.

Successively, examples of positive forbidden fruit would include such things as: a good understanding of reproduction and multiplication, praise and worship (as patterned by

God continuously Ps. 150), service to our fellow man, (all to the glory of God's holy name Gn 1:28). Love, goodness and the knowledge of craftsmanship (Ex 31:3), peace, long life, prosperity, success, good ego, recognition, good business transactions, excellence, health, promotion, enjoyment, tranquillity, sincerity, honesty, freedom, opportunity, song, dance, choice, protection, victory, acceptance, forgiveness, light, confidence, power, voice, fashion and many more, just to mention a few.

A Beginning to Everything

To everything God has created, there is a beginning. It is therefore noted that whatever you like too much, there lies within it the potential for allurement or ensnarement, to which one runs the risk of becoming a victim. For instance, the serpent was reported as being highly delighted, by Eve, in the garden amongst all the other animals. Unfortunately for her, the serpent was a subtle and flexible tool for Satan, by which to easily bring disruption, without even causing the smallest suspicion.

Already Satan the devil has said that he was going to make mankind go against the very will and purposes of God for their lives. He is so jealous of God's leadership that he attempted to rival it, which led him to being cast from heaven right down to earth.

The devil must have experimented with Eve, to discover what she liked most. In fact, Eve was his original target, simply because a man does not possess a womb so as to be able to carry a baby in order to fulfil God's pronouncement in Genesis 1:28.

The Womb was always Satan's Original Target

Adam was in the garden of Eden for a number of years without any error of sin against God. Besides, no child was ever added to him. It must be this woman that would complete him in order to birth God's expectation from mankind, concerning the replenishment of the entire earth, by humans.

He had to fight the woman, and succeeded by making everyone hostage to his kingdom, as though he were our judge. Yet we thank God, who came down in the form of Jesus Christ, in order to redeem mankind of their sins and for reconciliation to be made for our salvation. The bible says, "For God so loved the world, that He gave His only begotten Son, that whosoever believeth in Him should not perish, but have everlasting life" (Jn 3:16).

The choice, which we were all lured by the general accuser of the brethren, Satan, through the first parents (Adam and Eve), brought a total damnation and condemnation as a result. Yet by God's infinite mercy, the atonement of Jesus Christ saw us through. Glory be to the Lord God, as today we all have a hope of eternity, that is if someone believes in God through Jesus Christ our Lord as their personal Saviour, then he or she is saved. God has said: "I will have mercy on whom I will have mercy" (Rom 9:15).

The End of all Tribulations

The second coming of Jesus will definitely end all tribulations. And God's dealings with each individual personality is totally different from the other, because He can distinguish. The simple truth is that, there are no two persons with one destiny. If you like, falsify issues, it just can't work. The issue is that you remain completely your distinctive self, as you were made by God.

Jacob tried it, it didn't work. Even at the long run, having suffered the consequences, the whole thing bounced back to the true owner, which was Esau.

CHAPTER 14

Love of Stature

Full Distinction

Gorgeous ladies with small or average heads, including pointed noses, are very much welcome in here. She must be oblong or rounded face etc. This is full of distinction among the human race, as regard to these sets of people practising this type of love. You are underrated mostly when your height does not meet up with their requirement. Giant with huge and bulky-men are mostly the sets of men, tall, handsome, with average or relatively small head a man is welcome here.

Stature is very much invoked to men in our society. They are used as bodyguards. When eminent people like presidents, governors and others are going by, they mixed with the securities as entourages. Even in a profession like the navy, they are mostly particular about employing huge, bulky, hefty men due to the activity involved in the duty and other forces partially or relatively do same.

Keeping in Shape is Expected

In the Western world, if not globally, it is mostly recommended that both sexes should try to maintain a flat tummy, for many reasons, which can help the individual person in question. For this reason, so many people are into sports, physical fitness, gymnastic, and other exercises. Any lady with a quality outfit, attracts men so much.

Apart from that, being moderate in stature is very good also both for fabric and in posture. These people have great advantages against those who are fat, since they have problems with bodily fitted clothes. The moderately slim are used for fashion and adverts.

Ladies mostly like men that are tall, huge, or with average height and moderate stature, for husbands. It's relatively believed that such men have the ability for a physical protection on them. Besides, they're also presentable. They are advantageous in many areas against the fat ones, who are often lazy. And in presentation, they are more or less considered older than their ages.

Most of the so called ladies with this notion at the back of their minds, even when they have nothing in common with you, merely see how they take a twice glance at you, you can as well guess even relatively close to accurate what they got in their minds towards you.

Shoes always have Sizes

Some persons are slim or even very slim. Most fat men delight on ladies with this body structure. As slim men look for fat or average fat ladies, and fat men look for slim ladies and verse versa. Shoes, they say, have sizes. Short people are still very much useful on their own. They aren't lazy. In everything they do, they usually do with smartness. They look social and classic in appearance.

A fellow once asked he didn't know why each time he moved out with his younger brother, people seemed to respect the brother than him, the elder? Except those who knew them so very well back home, every other person hardly distinguished their respect as it ought to be. According to him, his brother was tall and handsome; a good looking guy, whilst he was moderately short with a baby face and stature. The answer is vivid; one you aren't very tall and secondly you carry a baby face.

The Respect of Physical Appearances

Really, we humans respect the physical appearance (even the height of persons). The disadvantage on the big people, is that they can grow tired so very easily. They cannot undertake any hard job. They usually battle with half laziness and half smartness.

Critically viewed the percentages of people who are fond of looking for a quick way to success, the fat people take the greater part. Publicly, they just can't hide to do anything in a place where security is tight. Due to the attractive appearance they carry; opportunity to embark on negative business without being noticed, is lagging on their part (identifiable mark). Which could be one of the disadvantages to the fat and tall people.

For that reason, they are mostly the ones buying the law enforcement agents, with authority, in order to freely embark on naughty business like: pushing of hard drugs, selling of cocaine, marijuana, and others. They kill people like fowls just to have their way, in case of any disruption to their intentions. The majority of them are typically merciless to the core, like the devil incarnate.

I am not against their natural endowment as far as stature is concerned, but I implore you as a rational fellow to take a closer look particularly at the fat people in movies, which portray the addictive crimes in society and tell yourself what you see.

❖

CHAPTER 15

Love of Womanising

The Weak-point of Lust

L ove of woman is natural. There is no law against being in genuine love with a single lady as a single young man. And it is commonly found among men, as the opposite sex, by nature. The bible records that a woman was formed with a rib from the side of a man and a man was the direct image from the Lord God Almighty Himself (Gn 2:22). So, that is the origin of the intimate relationship that exists between them, right from age.

Satan has also intelligently passed through this process, in order to make some men (whose week-point is the lust of women), victims of his strategic attack. What he does is to attack them spiritually, in order to lure them into it, in such a way, that they now are winning more souls to the kingdom of darkness. Unfortunately, if God does not intervene in such lives, the act could serve as opposition to their destinies for their entire lives. Somebody can be a tool for the devil and not even know it.

A Tool for the Devil

How? Because womanising is a weapon of the flesh, which certain powers can stir up to abuse the possessed, except by God's intervention. In getting their free way through this process, they take it as pleasure. It also gives them pride in catching their fun through it. Somebody doesn't wakeup, only to lust after women. Tracing the root to its cause, you find out that something must be wrong somewhere. Either the fellow is cursed or is suffering from an injured root or faulting foundation from long ago.

Anybody with this type of problem, doesn't just fornicate but also sleeps with other people's wives; worst of all sleeping with their own blood, without even feeling guilty or having any conscience about it at all. Isn't that surprising? May the good God have mercy.

On the other hand, it could be their choice, from the spiritual realm, I mean, the kingdom of darkness. As we all know, the choice you make determines your doings. If a fellow is not cursed, he/she cannot commit adultery. It is a trap that catches those with whom the Lord God is angry (Prv 22:14).

As the world develops, people became highly inclined with mental civilisation especially in the area of money; to the extent that family members fight one another.

Embarking on Evil Business

Spiritual and physical trade: in business and in slavery, have now become the order of mans days. Then Satan has soiled the heart of men, by making them desire the act of embarking on evil business.

Spiritually, the devil devours the riches of man through women. As nobody likes hardship, therefore, let the wealth be in the oven of anything called woman, any concerned bad guy or man is desperate to have it or collect it. Such people could slept with their own mothers and sisters, for whom they no longer care. Besides, they also take to fashion by having as many women as possible.

They so much believe in popularity through this process. They use it to intimidate their equals, to ridicule them to scorn and regard them as inferiors. On the other hand, it could also mean fooling their age-mates; whom they feel they are wiser than. Many people are into it for one reason or the other.

The majority designed this process or channel, in order to retaliate for what others have done to them before. Girlfriends, fiancées or wives are the concerned persons in this circle. They believe in using this method to satisfy their conscience over the hurt that they got from their evil neighbours. It also brings disaster. As the fellow who allows anger to lead him into sin might not find it so easy to make a return for a genuine repentance out of the shackle, hence a part of his character is even addicted to it.

The Result could be Drama

Just like too much sugar destroys the human system, he could either get a disease through it or have the wrong lady like him some how. And that could probably be the result he gets as a reward for the atrocities he has committed. It is also an expression of deep feelings of strong emotion. A particular rich man could be so resistant that any intimate relationship or attempt to toast his daughter might induce you with some kind of embarrassment.

So, the only way you could express your feelings of being insulted by the attitude of the father towards your being in contact with the daughter, is to use the girl and dump her. And that is too wrong to be done of any fellow, if really you are rational. Or maybe she personally decided to stress you on her own thinking; the result could be drama.

Some guys cannot take this insult and then just let it go like that, instead, they will want to tell the girl that all snails possess the same water and even at that, the sizes can never be the same ever. Actually in that cycle, the bad guys do know what to do in order to satisfy their flesh with some retaliations.

❖

CHAPTER 16

Influential Love

Self Aggrandisement

There are people who are just after making friendships with influential people in our society. All they are after is to be close to popular people in a big position and in higher class. They believe identifying with famous people is enough for their self aggrandisement. And some other advantages, like toasting girls they would never get to talk to, without such influence.

Such people — to the lovers of popularity — are good for a defence. Mostly when their voices are heard by the public, they are delighted with immediate effect. They also believe that when they're close to them, they'll be aided with assistance from them, wherever necessary. Although, not all

95

rich people are generous, a few are (while others are very stingy).

It is actually a thing of great pleasure for a very wealthy or notable figure in society to pay a visit to a very poor person. Before the surrounding neighbours, he or she feels great and highly honoured. The light of the presence of a wealthy personality has shone on them that day, whether or not anything comes out of it, still it is great and he feels honoured. Even an intimate greeting that they both share is something worth more than gold.

The Influence of Affluence

The presence of an affluent person means a total different atmosphere entirely, for the concern bodies. A stubborn child that is so arrogant could be referred to a rich family friend, by the parents, to speak to him or her in order to make a change for the better and turn up a new life. Before you know it, humility becomes the result. It could be due to the assistance given to the family by the rich personality. Even police like rich people as well.

They are aware that each time the chief is passing by them on the road-block, he must drop something to sustain the boys. Similarly, if it happens that anybody is arrested by them, it is related to and made familiar to the chief; they know that they are very lucky. Bribes makes some police like wealthy people in our society. Besides, they are usually humbled and cool and as a result their cases are usually easy for them to handle or deal with.

Apart from that, people like the influential people because they are very good in taking vengeance or in retaliating against opposition. Due to that fact, they believe moving closely to them could yield them with some help or rather give them a kind of privilege or influence to deal with their enemies. The authority of any rich person is humanly a big deal. If possible, can even help to humble your enemies.

❖

CHAPTER 17

Love of Notable Figures

Who Command Respect

These are simply referred to as the heads of every organisation such as: the music industry, of cults, the general public, political figures, and more. Most of the things that concern them, they serve somehow as consultants to those that are also concerned. Traditionally and culture, their royal appearance commands respect from people around them. They are crowned to their families as well as they are to the nations.

If you talk of pride, they are also reckoned with by the nation they hailed. They are even a pride to their nations themselves due to their professions. Many are stars whose careers have taken their nations up so very high. And for this simple reason, their governments do not joke with them also.

Influence can Corrupt

Due to their influence, their close people, get a kind of nepotism as an indirect benefit from them. Some so called humanly regarded smart guys, can use their name or influence alone to woo their lovers as girlfriends and even gain one or two things as help from other people. They can even marry with the name of their persons on this level. They serve them as an umbrella, for protection and defence against enemies.

The only problem is that such humanly estimated influence can corrupt a nation if care is not taken. Take for instance, you use your influence to secure a job even without merit, (the prerequisites and qualification for the job). I tell you, trust me, he or she is a complete ravaging disease to that company and in the nearest future if not inspected will affect the pulse of the federal government indirectly.

This is the reason why in some developed nations, scanning and screening are carried out year in and year out in companies by the inspectors of work, to ensure that the mediocre are filtered or better still they go for training in order to match with their required standard.

Some directors are happy with unskilled labours. Why? Because they are cheap to produce goods and services. Unskilled labour can accept to undertake any black job. Just because it is all about the income, they will no longer consider the risk of casualty, which will be overlooked without compensation if the need arises. Even with or without contract, unskilled labourers accept jobs provided there is payment.

Without the Fear of getting Caught

Some companies with nominal partners take the risk without fear of being caught. The directors know that they can't go to jail, due to the illegal authority backing them up. Any of these acts are worth doing, yet when it becomes too much, it can relegate the nation of her yearly income. That is why one cannot blame the federal government from doing anything possible by law to stop it; otherwise, it can affect you and me if not checked.

Many today are indulging into black jobs, black businesses and black markets; everything black, just to be able to dodge tax. If we don't pay tax, where on earth do you expect the government to generate resources to finance her projects for the benefit for the nation? So, please, let's do something for good, according to our societal conformity, else we are all heading nowhere.

❖

CHAPTER 18

Love of Names

Popularity and Star Recognition

There is no born element that doesn't want to make name for itself. The yearn of talented persons is to be highly respected; famous with a great population of fans; over popularity in short by name. A man's gift will make way for him, if carefully catered for and continually dwelt on for a very long time with persistence, popularity is sure. It is one of the incentives, otherwise the sacrifice is to no purpose.

Tell me why would a student burn candles, when the interest is not high on the certificate or degree that he or she is going to merit at the end of the day? Position can also determine how much you will be known or recognised. Obama was not able to merit his dignity of presidency before his presidential seat as the formal President of United State of America. But during his tenure and afterwards, he became very popular and highly esteemed by men. Though as an ordinary man, he must have earned some respect beforehand, but not to that same degree of recognition.

People of Different Calibres

Somebody is a star. Yes, someone is an important figure. God made it. Someone is even a ladder, somehow, somewhere. Someone is a bedsheet. Someone is clothing over nakedness. How? Because you get to know it when you begin to see people of different calibres.

We all are useful to one another. Slippers protect the bottom of your feet, while clothes cover your nakedness. You can see the value of your artificial possessions, not to mention your natural endowments. Be blessed and also be thankful to God.

If you have records in economy, you are bound to be recognised worldwide. It is known by its name, through production marks. And if from time to time, the company also embarks on public advertisement of its products, in order to create awareness, you may also be featured.

Generosity is very good also and that can also make one to be well known, more also if you are able to do it by extending it to orphanage homes. Right from the foundation or during our patriarchs, people have always commended and yearned to know wealthy personalities.

There are people who just have natural influence being endowed to them by God. Whatever help, you ask from them, they will definitely connect you to your helper. For this reason, they become much more known and even recognised by men. Obedience and respect are part of what can easily be worn by you, as a name that is directly due. As no condition is a permanent one, those who were forgotten as a result of their problems, will be known and remembered once again.

Lineages

There are some lineages who teamed-up right from the time they started bearing a single surname. And so, the more population there is, the more popular the name becomes. For example: Okojie, Okpere, Ibadi, Asemota and many more, just to mention a few. Many people get to marry up to as many as ten wives. Since this will entail having many in-laws, which will make such a fellow and family to be well known — in all these places that the wives belong and beyond — hence an outstanding name.

Chieftains and titles obtained from different places can also make names. Wealth is also talking or has voice in all these areas. The stars and other professionals have names easily spread all over, due to their professions. Secondly, if you are well learned you will be known as well. Some people because of a search for fans, decided to give themselves nick-names in order to become popular too.

However hard they try, it cannot really be successful; instead it can only end up making them known by a very few people around them. In a similar case, it is also what makes some people deliberately become awful and notoriously marked as deadly; thinking that will make them become very popular; not knowing that evil does not reign to last long.

Stigma: No Sore - No Flies!

Really a few persons could be well known and noticed inflicting people with certain bad sicknesses. Whatever you do, is what you are known for. Even if you are a bad business fellow or personality like the 419 just to confuse, cheat and loot people of their wealth, that is what you will be known for. Good or bad, names must have a foundation. And so, don't be surprised about someone with a stigma. Such is life.

Apart from the little we have discussed about names so far, the name you give to your children also matters a lot. Names can make someone become so arrogant for the rest of their lives, if God does not intervene. Names have so much to do with one's destiny, believe it or not. So, before even you give a name to your child as any parent, please, try and check to know the meaning and the meaning must be good. Stop using the intonation or sound that a name makes when it is spoken; for nature does not eat grammar. In a nut shell a word is enough for the wise.

To finally crown it all, you can become optimally popular by making God your Lord and personal Saviour. I pray for somebody, any name you bear, which has an inward negative impact on your life, must be scanned and screened with the blood of Jesus. No sore no flies.

❖

CHAPTER 19

Love of Good & Bad Names

Love of Good Names

Reputation and a good name is far more preferable than great wealth. A good name can even give you a good connection, which could result in an open door. This is because, people are just ready to meet famous people in person for that name alone. If you are naturally popular or influential, a good thing will always locate you.

A rich person could have money but he or she may lack the influence of good people to help them use the wealth judiciously, in order to minimise costs and maximise profits. And if they happen to locate you as a channel of opportunity, you are already a rich person (connected to greatness through influence); especially when they are the generous type. The difference will be if you meet a greedy fellow and you can understand what I am talking about.

It can give employment because you are a trustworthy person, with influence and sincerity. It brings breakthrough because you are well noted as a confiding person and as a result, nobody likes to obstruct or barricade you (meaning your way is always made straight and open). Since, if they ever do any business with you, the result is always accurate without cheating; so you have already won their hearts towards you with all honesty.

After all, that is what almost every global person is yearning for, in all circles; so your way is automatically pure. It can make you get so many friends, who love good things and like to identify with good things.

A Bad Name is like a Curse

Not until the name of brother Jabez: sorrow maker was changed for favour, he was never broken free from the shackle of limitation (1 Chr 4:9-10). Abram and Sarai got their names changed by God before even they gave birth to Isaac (Gn 17:5, 15) Jacob was not being receptive to the golden blessings of the Lord God in his life, not until God asked him, "What is your name?" He himself did not even know nor was he able to identify his problem (Gn 32:26-29).

A name can deal with you mercilessly and hide its identity so that you cannot provide a solution to crack the negative infect totally down. A bad name is like a curse. Anyone suffering from it is accused believe it or not. Please, before you give names to your children, make sure you know the meanings well. Otherwise, it is a ladder for the enemy to slow him or her down, if not completely stop them.

Love of Bad Names

In this world, it is either you are good or you are bad. A bad name can make way for you as well as a good name can. But one lasts more than the other. The truth is that one thing is sure that whatsoever a man sow that he shall reap. If you are the type who believes that doing people bad will always make them fear you—and engulf yourself with certain freedoms—rest assured that one day, you will end up with a disaster and become like a common animal.

If it is a good name, even at the beginning people may not bother to even recognise you. Some may even deliberately refuse to recognise you with it because they feel it has no benefit to yield them. Believe you me, at a time, it must surface such that you will last if not forever. It could make you get so many enemies, even hinder your way to success yet the Landlord—God of it, is simply and always with you.

The freedom you get with a bad name does not usually last long. The truth is that the foundation is fake and the action is fake and everything about the whole system is totally fake and as such it risks defeat to the end; until it totally fades away.

At the end you will be the one now looking for whom to identify with. Even your mind will condemn you in memory of those you've bruised and offended in the past with jeopardy and all that. Only God can then save you, that is if your getting fed up with evil and bad dealings is genuine in the sight of the Lord God.

Genuine Repentance

That is if your sudden repentance is genuine from the inn and is confirmed from the root of your heart that you will no longer harbour failing/disappointing people in your container. If your cry is a genuine intention to repent and stop your ritualism and to stop your negative indulgence. And if it is a stop to your perpetrator.

And that is if your sorry is a complete stop to your sleeping with your neighbour's wives. That is if your intention is a no to betraying and frustrating people. That is if your confession is a complete no to your being judgmental. That is if it is a complete cut down to your undue ego. If it is a no to intimidation and wrong laughter/gloating on your neighbour's drastic curriculum.

Heaven made people to know that you are fierce; it will now begin to serve as a coverage for you to indulge in crimes with boldness. Bad character intoxicates, even more than alcoholic drinks. Evil powers made it by carefully injecting their targeted victims, in order to spoil their characters.

Similarly, if you also disregard His Sovereignty, He will spoil your mind and character to begin to misbehave to embarrass yourself before people. Who does not know can never know. It is a secret only God can reveal when He means to do it through the person of the Holy Spirit and the issue concerns the deliverance department in the church of Jesus Christ to be made manifest. It is never the fault of a common man to see a situation and condemn the victim instantly.

Bad People cannot be Trusted with Good Things

A carnal man can never understands the things of the spirit. Some notorious guys in this class use it as an opportunity to rape girls whom they feel have no solid persons to take on vengeance against them. They can locally steal with it. They could even be assassins not mind making it even pronounced to people around them so that they can begin to fear them.

This bad name can attract occultism and that will force agents to join with their group in order to assist in the activities or they themselves could voluntarily decide to join in order to go about bragging with the identity and mark. Some elements do intimidate with the mark of their fraternity. They strongly believe they got the ultimate power, which can take them to the top most. An umbrella with fake authority! It is like some men are under compulsion; honestly. May the good God help them.

Fake identity and fake recognition, what a life! Such people are easily known by their attitude towards elders anywhere, anytime, any day and any moment. The evil spirit doesn't allow the possessors to respect their elders and good authority. It makes the agents to believe that even when they are wrong, they could still be right, and when they are even right they are the ultimate. Humility is with those that believe in this authority. Perversions and injustices are the order of their days to the core. If you therefore leave leadership to the hand of these people, they will rot lives by turning the world completely upside down. Bad people cannot be trusted with good things.

❖

CHAPTER 20

Love of Trouble Making

Indulging in Crimes

Trouble is just like a food to some people. As bad as trouble is, you can't imagine someone likes it. They believe it will help them to gain ground and freedom from opposition and even serve them with the opportunity to indulge in crimes and get away with it. Similarly, that it will help to defend their ground for anything at all.

If anybody hears about them therefore, he or she will be scared of them even when yet to surface in person. And so, they simply resign to embarking on what will make them put on fierce appearance by taking hard-drugs and smoking marijuana. Trouble is not in anyway a good thing or a reputation to any rational being; nor even love to possess either; yet some people like it.

Now, illiterate people are mostly fond of doing things as to know if they could use it as an opportunity to indulge in one or two things, which on a neutral ground his or her qualifications can't take them there. They are very many. You can find them in the leadership, in family, in company, in nations, and in group. On the other hand, a troublesome person could be living in a curse who knows? It is accursed to live like that. May God deliver somebody in Jesus' name.

The atmosphere in an egg is quite different from the open air on the space by the embryo. It is equally so with bad people, not until the dangerous truth with the unquenchable light of God enters them, they will not know they have been in darkness. May the genuine deliverance of God save you under such a pressure with shackles in Jesus' name.

❖

CHAPTER 21

Love of Violence & Rebellion

Intolerance and Disobedience

Lack of tolerance can be regarded as violence. While rebellion is an act of disobedience to law and order. There are so many reasons why people decide to become violent. You find out that a fellow could be gentle and soft, humble and cool on his own; someone somewhere from the blues will still look for a way in order to stir up anger in him by sissy.

For being taken as a coward, he would want to do something in order to prove to them—not that he can't revenge or retaliate—it's just that he never wanted to do anything silly or nasty, which was why he kept quiet in the first place.

As if that was not enough, on seeing you, some bad ones who felt that they possess the white teeth, will resign to ridicule you to scorn. Such ground could call for trouble. The fact that you are a human being does not give you a complete right to rubbish the joy of your neighbour and then expect to be welcomed; no never. Remember, even besides the federal constitutions, individuals are endowed by God with weapons of self defence. And so, be careful how you treat your neighbour.

There's no Gain in Arrogance

Primarily, I dare you to take a critical look at the animals in the open field. What do you think is the meaning of their teeth being given to them by God; is it for eating alone? Oh, never, spare me of your indifference to the truth here. Their horns etc., are for a defence. Owing to that, you can as well think of humans, the kind of reactions as an expression towards unbearable situations by humanity and some oppressions.

So, please shun your so called negativity, which could call for an action or even a reaction. I do suppose life is sweet and beautiful for us all. I don't know how it is with you, but I would that we all enjoy life to the fullest. Okay. This is my feelings rather than engaging in the act of a melodrama. I pray you get informed beforehand, that in life, there is no gain in arrogance.

Any student that went to school, by all means, I do mean with all his little effort, as he came out without job and can't afford to remain a liability, will want to resign to robbery in order to recover his money.

You don't Force Love

Or a person who feels they're too intelligent, and so cheat on you and if there is no other means to deal with such a fellow, other than to rob him or her in order to recover your money or property as the case maybe; he simply does it straight away. This is possible with the doers because they've not seen the light yet. They are in no doubt believers of the Mosaic law: tooth for tooth, eye for eye.

Some elements believe in taking by force. And so, if they toast any girl they like and she just does not accept their proposal, they think the only thing they should do is to rape her. You don't force love. Any love making under force can never be enjoyed.

Illiterate and demonic influence are what worry people like that. Imagine who does not have interest in you even in his or her mind pertaining to love, is it when you now force her that she can gladly accept? No, never. Have you ever noticed how illiterate some people are that are so very violent? Even in leadership.

More or Less Dictators

Politically they hardly — if at all — accept objection, interference or even a correction from anybody. They act like Napoleon to laws already made in order to suite their doings without being questioned to order. They are always more or less dictators. They usually do things anyhow. If you correct them in order to be skilled in working places, they will either confront you with the saying: "I know" or even carry some grudges against you.

In school, they are ready to prove the teacher wrong with a fake private research that they've made. They always disobey orders and yet claim to be right. Most of the riots that have ever taken place, are usually responsible by them.

In attempt to carry out a demonstration, which when critically analysed is full of negativity, you find out their hand is not far from it. When agitation does not follow the right source or carry the action with normal procedure, it becomes a rebellion to the eyes of the viewers and a disobedience to law and order of wheresoever is done.

Retaliation

Individually, a person can retaliate because he or she is bruised. Some use acid or even engage in physical combat to express their feelings of being hurt and tired, even fed up with oppression and that they just can't continue to condone it any more.

Spiritually, some elements retaliate against their neighbours, which they find a thorn in their flesh. Some unbelievers fight back in order to secure themselves against a kind of spiritual threat. But as for the believers, the bible says, we wrestle not against flesh and blood but against powers and principalities in high places (Eph 6:12).

❖

CHAPTER 22

Love of Fight

Trouble Makers

Some persons are street obtuse. Their belief is that, they are the alpha and omega and so they will always want to taste their physical energy, which they so trust and relied on. In reverse, it may not necessarily be that he or she wants to test his physical ability but rather for freedom and for a defence.

The world is so full of strongholds. Besides spiritual troubles, certain elements will still want to bring their riding over you from the secret spiritual realm into physical realm, which your humanity may not take or condone for goodness sake; except by Christian faith that you carefully put it under control with prayers to the God of vengeance to help fight for you (Ps 94:1).

It is not as if you have been trained or you wanted to test your strength; though some people do that anyway. But in case it comes your way, you fight to defend yourself. For example, Christians can never relent to be defeated in their spiritual battles of life to victory to eternity. So, see to that yourself and then know how you go about your case.

Power tussles love to fight whether or not you offend them. In short, they are just trouble makers. They so trust their artificial means by which they highness their physical powers. Some are even trained to become bold and energetic. They either smoke marijuana, hard-drugs, or swallow other powerful tablets.

Fighting Destroys so many Things

Agents of the devil purposely love fighting the peace makers—Christians everywhere—in order to receive promotion from Satan their master. There could be powers in the form of personalities, random others, or worst of all one's own people (Mt 10:36). Because they are possessed by evil spirits, they can't undo to accomplish their missions. If it is a task to fulfil before promotion can take place, therefore, anybody in charge can do it; even take it as a task with a done issue.

Fighting destroys so many things. It can scatter any relationship and create enmity including disunity. It is a revenge; or a retaliation against what has happened before, probably by someone else, which he or she did not like. Some express their feelings by fight over a girl they toasted that refused their proposal. But fighting anyone over her refusal to your proposal just doesn't make any sense.

Love is Unforced

There is nowhere on earth you can force love and succeed — never — it doesn't exist. If you are the type that forces people to love you, you are making a hell of mistakes. Let me tell you, you are just forcing to insert yourself into them, in order to be loved. But unfortunately they don't even have love for you; what they have they must give to you (hatred).

In case you don't know, that is why if you release positive, you get negative. You sow good but get bad and vice versa. Love is like nature itself and so let it be as it is before you regret your deed. May that not be somebody's portion in Jesus' name.

Forcing someone to like you, is the equivalent of inviting an enemy into your life. Look, he or she doesn't have your love. And of course, you know that if one does not have this, they will definitely have that. What he has he will give to you. Be careful, all that glitters is not gold.

CHAPTER 23

Love of Peace

You can Never Unite without Love

When you make peace, peace will definitely follow you to wherever you go and even abide with you. Peace stimulates unity and co-operations no doubt. You can never unite without love. And love is capable of solving all kinds of problems. It can even move mountains. A mountain could be any problem. It can cure all manner of sicknesses and diseases like: HIV/AIDS in a positive state. It can even alleviate poverty and bring riches.

Love is a healing medicine, which you can't buy in the chemist or supermarket. It can cover multitudes of sins and thereby birth harmony, which money cannot buy. Nothing forces love to come. It operates wilfully and comes from the wilful heart of whom it abides. One cannot love truly without obeying.

Anyone that makes peace, is a child of God. God likes peace as well as man. Where there is peace, you can never see anyone drawing heat and striving with each other. Tranquillity usually becomes the MC, as the order of the day. God is the leader wherever there is peace. Therefore, unity, co-operation, obedience, tranquillity, and many more are children of love.

With a true love, the world does not need even a judgement. If it is possible, live peacefully with all men. For a true love has no charges against it. Nothing barricades you from whom you love or like when it comes to approach for anything good. It could be begging for alms or any kind of assistance. The nature of brotherhood can never function or be exercised without this true love in question.

Evangelism Flows with Love

Evangelism flows with love. You can even win your people first of all to Christ even before any other person out there. No doubt, that is to tell you that the foundation of each ministry begins from home. But the fact that love is generally declared harmless doesn't mean you should get carried away without applying wisdom. Things could change at times. The devil is wicked and at the same time trickish. And so, you must be vigilant (2 Cor 2:11).

Jesus, in the form of human nature, did not say to himself, *"Ah my Father will protect me,"* and then played along with

Satan. Instead, He carefully applied the wisdom of God, in conjunction with the word of knowledge (bible) to beat his temptation to condemnation. If Jesus is your role model, you must use the same thing in order to defeat your tempters in Jesus' name. Our tempters are not far from us.

❖

CHAPTER 24

Love of Comfort & Relaxation

Love of Comfort

Everybody likes a state of comfortability. If it were buyable, people would definitely buy it; provided it is just okay by them. But it is very much unfortunate that you just can't buy it. It is simply natural. It is only God that can give it to the needy. Comfort is not all about the amount of wealth a man has acquired to him or herself, rather it is determined by the percentage of freedom the Lord God has given to an individual personality to enjoy.

In the school of comfort, everybody wants to wild-up on spaces, without any disturbance from anybody. You would want to live in a very specious compound in which there is a big building that belongs to you as your personal property or asset. The compound must be well tied and stocked up with different brands of cars and jeeps.

Secondly, you would want a situation whereby there is a supermarket in your compound, two toilets and two bathrooms, with televisions in each. You would want to own a multimillion investment of your own in which people are working for you. Your own is only to carry out private inspections, which is usually done occasionally. To attain this giant, you must know there are many rivers to cross. So, I leave that with you.

When you really have these, according as it pleases your mind, you will notice that you suddenly begin to grow fat. It is never the whole things you get now that are responsible for your level of comfortability, rather it is the inner result, which you got at the end of the day and must manifest itself to the outward visibility of mankind. You just don't know this time around nor how it comes, neither can you stop it but just simply flowing as the Master—God has allotted it (Jer 29:11). So, take it and enjoy it to His glory in Jesus' name.

Love of Relaxation

This is a love of taking a rest, which at times may just be the result of a long hard day on the job. It could be on a relaxation post or even at home. If you have taken a very long walk for a journey, you are expected to take a rest in order to gather momentum just to keep it on, until you actually get to your destination.

The Israelites, according to ancient history, were reported to have travelled by foot 40 years in the wilderness.

Whenever they where tired, they stopped and took some few days, weeks or even months of rest and then picked up and started going on their journey until they finally got to the promised land of (Canaan).

Not only time to rest but also time to take some refreshment and delicacies or delicious meals and to reason deep as well, is vitally important to the human body. Depending on how one plans it. You can have it as good time or otherwise. Work per se, does not end one day. Instead of working all days in your lives, the government has created a room whereby according to each worker's contract, a worker is entitled with some number of days in every months for a rest; in order to avoid being bored.

Good Health Fuels & Oils Enthusiasm

Someone may work and work just to pursue wealth and then die to leave the wealth behind at last for whom doesn't even know how he or she suffered to acquire such wealth. Make money and use it to enjoy your life also; else you die and leave it for whom never witnessed how you suffered for it.

Everyday enjoyment is very important. One could ask how is that possible? One has actually asked well. It is very very possible by daily feeding on good food in time while you are on your daily routes. I knew at the first sight of these few lines of words, your mind flew because you weren't having a quick clue to grasp what it means. I can even feel it from your breath right now that someone somewhere is already doing it even without knowing it.

I dare you to keep it up for it will definitely help you to go a long way. Take proper care of yourself even before any other thing. When there is life, there is hope. Let health be your propeller besides that from God in doing anything.

Health is the number one engine that fuels or oils your enthusiasm to do any job, day in and day out. As the struggle of human beings continues till death, you must schedule yourself in accordance to your daily routines for a success by you. Take your blissful days in Jesus' name.

❖

CHAPTER 25

Love of Happiness

In God Alone

This is a sort of feeling, a stage in life of having nothing to worry about over one or two things. It could be lucky of a position, how you feel in health and in all ramification, thought, success, celebration, satisfaction, pleasure, willing and suitable to your desirable standard.

Happiness is very important. Every living thing including man from A – Z needs it. Happiness is free. It is naturally given by God. There is no supermarket where on earth it is bought and sold. If at all, it must be labelled with an expiry date. Meaning you are therefore, expected to renew it as soon as possible.

The moment you default or fail to do so, there comes sadness. It is simply natural, with only one source, which is God Himself. You could drink the highest wine, smoke the most valuable cigarettes, play melodious music, eat all kinds of collective sweet foods and expect to get joy or happiness; only to be surprised that none of those can really do it as actually expected by you.

You could make a huge sum of money or even win a substantial amount of money from a lottery, which may probably soar you so very high; all together this cannot succeed in giving you the actual maximum percentage of happiness required by you. The fact that you have done all the whole of the above analyses doesn't make you a happy person. Except in God can you find true lasting happiness; even if sin shatters it, it can still be restored after being forgiven by the Sovereignty.

True Happiness Adds Weight

A true happiness can make you fat by adding more weight to your weight; otherwise, not even your so called daily pleasure and flexing can do that for you. It brings you with comfort, anytime, any day and any moment; followed by peace and tranquillity. When it overwhelms an individual in the mood, in fact, he or she becomes a friend casually with almost everybody, just like water without enemy.

If care is not taken, he or she begins to discharge respect to both young and old, without proving any sign of superiority. And it is researched with proof that if you work for the pursuit of happiness it is likely that you are selfish in that you may not get it or rather end up damaging your relationship with some other people. The simple fact is that they feel your feelings and they don't even know how you feel nor how it is with you.

Happiness & Forgiveness make you Appear Younger

You can see the logic. And if you take a critical look at people who are always happy, they usually appear younger everyday mostly on their facial looks. An overwhelmed conscience with happiness does not always remember any wrong being done to it by anyone. To crown it, forgiveness is always the answer. You will gladly appreciate when all of a sudden you find yourself dwelling in the midst of your desirable people and that desire you too.

If changing your old friends for new ones will make you happy, I would definitely advise you to do so. Everybody cannot be your friend; never, no, never. God the Creator of heaven and the earth did not have all the whole angels in agreement with Him! If you are a Christian, someone somewhere hates you. If you are truthful, you are hated by those that do not love truth. If you are light, lovers of darkness will say they just don't want to set eyes on you.

The fact is that, if you come, they can't exist anymore. If you are just or you are a lover of justice, agents of perversion hate you completely with a passion. Jesus was an example of the dangerous truth with unquenchable light; such as the time He ran away through a midst of the throng, when they were about to stone Him, because He spoke the truth (Jn 10:39).

THE HEART OF LOVE

Who are you as any Christlike that some people will not hate who have allowed the devil to soil their mind against truth and justice? Believe you me, such people are suffering from spiritual dullness. They are even bewitched in the sense, they can only see truth as lie and lie as truth. Trust me if you perverse, punishment encroaches at your door no doubt. It must happen because it is a law of nature by God and so, it is non-evadable. May God deliver us in Jesus' name.

Love of Tranquillity

Everybody wants a quiet life full of peace. From government: I do mean nation to the least of every living thing, like a state of peace and quietness. Even animal families are also included in these wants and desires. No species wants animal from another spacey to jump into their midst just like that; which is either to scatter or to kill as a predator or even as a carnivorous or a scavenger. Some animals are lovely while some are just hostile.

Human beings from his or her foetus, to adult stage, even unto death, do not want any kind disturbance. You want peaceful lives, as well as I want. But surprisingly, this is not usually the case of the matter this day; in the sense, invaders are too much. Whether you like it or not, they forcefully carry out their activities against your life in the name of collective powers in your bad society (fraternity).

They set all kinds of due and undue traps to entangle you, in order to track you completely down, just to force you to succumb to their so called evil reigning ways. And as an ignorant, you may take an oath on behalf of your family due to your level of understanding about her and how you grew up to meet it in the act of unity. But behold, little did you know that your so called exemplary family is on global societal network on the basis of evil; and that demonic influence is even remote-controlling her.

Every family belongs to a society, whether you like it or not. How does your curiosity begin? My friend, it is when you want to launch deep in life and you begin to experience some kind of snares that you become much more curious. Behold! When you watch very well, you can see that the curse is just around you. May God deliver someone in Jesus' name. *"It takes a strange thing to attract a research."*

Battles in the Home

Take for instance, a family will be very much united; loving, co-operative and interested in one another, but all of a sudden one happens to travel across the seashore. The moment he or she sends the first money to everybody in the family, you find out immediately that evil has entered the family and then stirred up battles in the home against one another. As if the devil was the owner of the money. If they where in good terms before, now the case will automatically be changed.

Discrimination, chaos and hatred will automatically become the order of their days. Why? The simple fact is that ones choice has automatically brought about a collective responsibility to every member in the family. Truth, love, interest, care, are all forgotten issues now because a bad fish has entered the water. Division, whether you like it or not, is written on the entrance to the family door. O! A sweet delighted home is now a horrible place. What a life!

Don't be afraid, for the bible says (Is 41:10). There is a reason why the Lord God ordained that you should be given birth to in that home. You are the light. And so, I dare you to change and correct the errors for light to the glory of God.

Light can never run from darkness; it has never been nor will ever be. No matter the number of times that light rises—it fails to even encounter failure—and raises again and again to beat the gravity of evil manifestations to the ground beneath the surface of the earth.

❖

CHAPTER 26

Love of Gentleness & Kindness

Taking things Calm and Cool

This is an act of doing in a quite careful way. It is also known as kindness. People with these characteristics are regarded as peace makers. One can even say they got it from God; since one of His attributes is kindness (Ps 91:14).

They just don't rush in anything they do but always take things calm and cool. Not that they are afraid of something but they are always very careful in their doings, in order to avoid being rash. They are gentle-jack; very cool to the core, no trouble, because they just do not want to harm you. Don't engage in a kind of forceful act with them; it could be a kind of trouble, which might result otherwise by them: trouble infinity.

A gentle person is highly more of privilege than any person. The simple difference is that the bad has already incurred disadvantage as a result of bad record. Stigma is a blockage. He or she could be allowed access to a place where others have restrictions, due to confidence people placed on him. Gentle people are obedient but don't mess with them. They just don't care even respecting their junior first but that doesn't mean you are asked to contract or step on their toes without even a cause.

They are reckoned with in humility; nor are they proud by carrying haughty looks in their appearance. In love, they are number one in the sense, almost all ladies would want to play with them simply because they are not porous.

Lucrative Cheating

It is a situation, which helps the ladies in their business of cheating. It is so very lucrative to them who are fond of dating more than one guy at a time. While guys with these characteristics also enjoy the best from ladies that care so much on their guys; in terms of buying material things and the giving of money and even expressing their feelings towards them also in kind. They don't stress before they get from whomever that is on this line of love, on that basis.

Do you know how many girls that have spent up to the amount worth to building an apartment for their guys? One, it is either they did it wilfully. Two, some could do it under compulsion by charm or trick. Some have even bought apartments for their guys, just to prove to them how much they care. Many have equally done without being appreciated.

Ungrateful is ever Ungrateful

However, they will never commit suicide no matter what. Ungrateful is ever ungrateful; that is the highest he or she can be and you can't change them. Some ingrates have thrown away guys or girls that have helped them during dark days in their lives. Now that it is bright on them, they just don't see anything good about them any more. Any element like that, do you think you are so very smart? It is never your smartness, rather your stupidity, to do that to your angel.

Many, as a result of this have possessed a mistake of wealth. But all the same, glory be to the God of justice who neither sleeps nor slumbers. In that He sees your situation, I do mean you in that pain. God will soon visit you and your life will change for the better. He is a God of restoration (Jl 2:25).

❖

CHAPTER 27

Love of Truth

The Key to Freedom

This is the positive aspect of any issue or matter. It is also known as justice that builds a nation. The bible says, the righteous are as bold as a lion (Prv 28:1). It happens as a result of the truth, which they know will always set them free (Jn 8:32). Jehovah Himself is involved and embedded in the truth that is why it can never die and what truth can do when it surfaces no one can quantify.

If you are a truthful person, you do not need a witness or even a defender nor even a lawyer in some cases. Except law demands that a lawyer must represent you whether or not you are right or even wrong. Truth can be regarded as a key to freedom. It brings a reliability, confidence and trust on someone. Truth per se, goes beyond the ordinary, much more than just oral.

Justified by the Knowledge of Truth

One can only be justified and purified by knowing the truth and practice it accurately. Law cannot say respect traffic and you beat it when driving and expect to be justified. You cannot hide to drive a car without an insurance contract, whereby law states that it is compulsory to insure your car for maintenance reasons, in case of necessities. You have not done any justice to the truth if you board any train or bus without a ticket.

Serve with humility and respect those in authority, by that you are justified. And that makes you much more a child of God, simply because you do not pervert justice, wherever you go and whatever you do. Your action teaches people nothing but the truth. A nation is built on a solid foundation of justice and fairness.

It helps to limit or minimise stress for judges or kings to have gone about as far as searching for more witnesses, even before deciding or presiding a case between two quarrelling persons are concerned, (so that he does not make any mistake), by passing a wrong judgement in favour of who does not merit it. It is therefore a short cut to settling issues peacefully.

If you know and understand the instruction of a job, it makes you skilled and that helps to facilitate the job. Truth can produce a genuine recognition and that can even make many people to start talking good about you. This is where the parable, *"a good name is rather to be chosen than great wealth."* You can take part in every confidential matter around you because you are just confided in by someone.

Truth has Consequences

Truth paves the way by connecting you to people that matter. Well, as we all know that the world is full of evil characters who are desperate to do, *"does and don'ts."* And due to that simple fact, truth now also has consequences such as: hatred, malice, attacks and many more just to mention but a few.

Truthful people aren't mostly wanted by awful people in our human society. We are in a world whereby eventually everybody believes in bad society and if you do not belong, your way to success is antagonised or barricaded. They will so abhor you that it will even cause you unemployment in your work place, even if you were working beforehand. In this case, truth has made you suffer poverty.

People who hate truth won't mind blackmailing you in order to make friends with people to desert you; and then make you become lowly. For example, a true love by Jacob (Israel) for Joseph brought hatred between Joseph and his brethren (Gn 37:2-11). It can make even your biological parents to disown you. Communal people can even ostracise you, mostly when the guilty are more influential than you are.

A wicked person can decide to level allegations against you before the elders in council, kings or leaders of a community, in order to have you totally banished from the village or place entirely.

Truth is dangerous and it possesses unquenchable light. It can make you go to jail and even be killed for it. However dangerous and risking it is, speak it, if you do have opportunity because God Himself is in it and who knows, that could be your ticket to the heavenly paradise. Truthful people are God's representatives; so be one.

CHAPTER 28

Love of Stubbornness

Just vs. Unjust Stubbornness

It is a rigidity of anyone not to succumb to order and instructions. Sometimes it is good and on the other hand, it's not good also. When you are stubborn against good, you can miss so much. But you can have freedom to some extent and also an access to so many things. Which in the real sense, the process is not going to be lawful because you are lawless. The simple fact is that negative can never access nor allow to get anything good either except by the other way round. You can do whatever you like with it.

Also there is good stubbornness. You can be stubborn against evil in that you don't accept nor side-part with evil and it is very nice. Such a just stubbornness is completely against any form of oppression and injustice even perversion. Even if the bad ones would want you to join them, you will never join because they are not doing the correct thing. It can induce you with easy breakthrough.

With this many people have chosen to live by violence, due to circumstances around them. And if care is not taken, it can make you even retaliate before the federal constitution. Behold! Punishment encroaches at the door of such a person and that could be the answer to such acts. The bible says that vengeance is God's (Ps 94:1).

Holding your Peace

My advice to you as anybody under trials and temptations is this; accept God as your Lord and personal Saviour and then leave your battle with Him, He will fight for you. Moses said to the Israelites, the Egyptians you see today, you shall see them no more, the Lord God will fight for you and you shall hold your peace (Ex 14:13-14).

If you were to fight for yourself, you may not really know whom your enemies are nor the tactics to apply in battling them away from your life. But God knows what, how, where and when to actually strategise, in order to hook your enemies till you are free. No matter what, don't take law into your own hands, there is still away out of that situation to avoid a disaster.

I do believe you don't want anything going *from the frying pan into the fire!* For God did not sanction nor approve that humans can begin to engage in physical combat when offended by a neighbour.

Be informed that we all wrestle not against flesh and blood but against powers and principalities in heavenly places (Eph 6:12). One can even avert trouble by prayer, even before it attempts to manifest, as projected by our enemies; by carefully following one's dreams systematically as they come. Those that work for the devil calculate the people of God every now and then.

Stubborn People are useful to Satan

Stubbornness can make bad people begin to disturb you, in order to join them by force into groups of fraternity. Your characteristics are serving them with an insight that you can serve as a tool to them on one or two missions. The truth is that, stubborn people are useful to Satan as agents of disruption and even for a destruction. Evil society needs people that are so very stubborn and hard hearted.

You can also lose genuine relationships because no responsible persons like to make friendships with hard hearted people, who are so very rigid to get along with (and those who have buried their human sympathy are not far from this also).

A wicked person has feeling but the problem is that the feeling is being anointed by evil power and as such now begin to produce negative results for those around them. Such a one can't be trusted, not even once, because he or she can just rise up overnight and display some stupid thing that you just can't believe. It is a complete chameleon by character; unreliable and unpredictable. And if it happens like that, it will become so very embarrassing.

147

Stubbornness can induce one with an early grave. Lions, tigers, hyenas, elephants, crocodiles and other wilds creatures, even pythons, do lose their lives to other dangers. Stubbornness is no guarantee. *"A dead wood is still surrendered to death in that it can still be used to kindle fire in order to do one or two things."* Disobedience is a complete bad name.

The Glory belongs to the Lord

Most ladies without conscience, believe in going out with humanly regarded strong men. For example, to them, it is a guarantee for their safety. Yet God has said in the bible that if you rely yourself on someone simply because he or she has power and he can use his or her physical strength to defend or rather protect you any how, any time, any day, is why you rely on him or her, that He — God would make him disappoint you (Is 31:1-3, Ps 118:8-9).

For example, Goliath really disappointed the army of the Philistines. You can say that again. At the end, they became prisoners of war. And so that induces more women on the person before you get to know of it, they will have ruined his life as a humanly regarded a powerful man or even a champion. To this end, the glory that belongs to God must never be given to any man.

❖

CHAPTER 29

Love of Smoking

Love of Smoking of Cigarettes

Cigarettes are the most common thing and some fashionable guys and even ladies indulge in smoking without even a cause. They believe that when they are at a party, to be loved is to hold a stick of cigarette on their lips or between their fingers. Similarly, they also do believe that smoking cigarettes can help alleviate some griefs in life.

Really we can't tell how it is with someone nor how life treats them. You and I can only tell a little based on sight and how an individual feels; more also with similar experiences. Meanwhile a lot is covered by clothes, even concealed up by the victim in question. Yes. You can say that again. Many are dying quietly in their closest. Only the Sovereign Lord can actually tell it all and Him alone has the solution to all problems. Jesus is the answer. I tell you.

An Opportunity to Waste Time

When they are offended, they resign to smoking cigarettes in order to cool down their temper and see if they can cope or induce themselves to forgive their offenders. A lot of habitual smokers have reported being able to surpass certain offences against them, which if retaliated, would have resulted into a disaster. Thanks be to God that I've got a control measure with which to regulate my anger; behold the reaction subsides.

Most of the companies that accept smoking of cigarettes do pave the way for sets of people who are relatively lazy to use it as an opportunity to waste time even during work hours and thereby short the director of his quota at the end of the day. When an impute does not yield the company with their expected results, then he or she is fired with immediate effect to avoid a diminishing return in the long run.

Really, some habitual smokers, over smoke, to the extent it is totally disgustful. Critically viewed from the source as a point of view, one will get to find out that it connects to spiritual activities by the concerned powers against their targeted victims. It is either they made that choice from the spiritual realm; as the only alternative means to saving their lives from danger or it was a devilish calculation to waste their resources, as life is more important than material wealth.

While on the other hand, some deliberately chose it purposely for the sake of negative business. In the institution, some popular people do believe that it helps them improve in assimilation and even improve their memory.

Due to all these beliefs that some people have towards cigarettes, the devil has a well developed process of extorting resources from habitual smokers; by making them to spend so much on cigarettes by advertisements carefully carried out to induce people with the interest. Since a lot of benefits have been attributed to it. We all know that extravagance reduces savings and wealth, which cigarettes have influenced.

The Best Wealth of a Man is his Health

You don't doubt a habitual smoker. Do you? Did I hear you say how? A smoking person usually goes with the odour of cigarettes. However clean and neat the person may appear to look in the very eyes of the onlookers, the strong odour defies their outfit. He or she is more or less a complete drunk alike. That identity follows them to wherever they go.

Research has proved that cigarettes contain nicotine. This of course could accumulate in the blood stream particularly the heart and lungs, which could in turn result to heart diseases. It can likely later also develop into Asthma and tuberculosis. Even when the federal government is campaigning against it saying: smokers are liable to die young, many are still adamant to do this. Smokers should be careful on how they go about smoking to risk their health. The best wealth of a man is his health, which is the foundation of all wealth.

Love of Smoking Marijuana

Herbs are good and medicinal. But not all are good in the body systems for a consumption. For example there's strong herbs like marijuana. Some elements even use it in making porridge, mixing drinks or soaking in water for a consumption or finally folded and smoked like a cigarette.

Some report that it gives them energy, which enables them to do an extra work load, which two people put together under normal conditions couldn't do. And bad people equally smoke it with a deliberate motive to fight their neighbours. While others smoke it to generate a long duration during sexual activity and many other motives.

Also, those smoking this marijuana are noted with specific traits or characteristics. For example they're usually mellow, tolerant and forgiving people (that's the good minded ones). Their gentleness is completely extra. If you shake their hands, it is usually soft and lukewarm and their lips are usually black in complexion.

An Artificial Power-Up

So many smoking guys complain of their inability to satisfy their ladies and as such resign to smoking marijuana in order to be able to stay longer and perform very well. It is an artificial power-up anyway. It has a limited duration after intake, after which the smoker returns to his or her former state of normalcy.

The question is this; does it work for everybody? The simple answer is no. Not everybody is the same. And so, the smokers can stimulate interest in sex. Some people mostly plant it in the farm while others trade it for money. During working hours, a worker that smokes it uses it to waste time and then rest unnecessarily.

The Dangers of Ignorant Imitations

Due to some of the advantages involved, those who smoke it, advertise to the ignorant (and whose blood could be different), and who would want to try it and experience how it is. However, blending with a new thing, of which one is not too sure (by imitation), is a total risk trust me. In the long run, it usually disappoints. Either the person begins to develop strange behaviours or it causes a very bad reaction.

Also it has a very bad odour, which makes its smokers easily recognisable and identified among other people in public. Some of these sets are cursed by it. It is a pity that some children that incarnated just yesterday are smoking it even today. If you ask them why, they answer and say it is the era of the new generation. Are we all crazy? To this end, life is totally questionable in some cases.

❖

CHAPTER 30

Love of Snorting Drugs

Peer Pressure & Indulgence

The modern age has brought about interests in addiction, which people embark on smoking or snorting in order to develop extra energy, for one or two activities with their reasons. It is a category of fashion. Peer pressure has birthed the majority of such indulgences. Power that one gets from this is for quick action, reaction and uses. It is either for sex to make a film or for personal private use in order to catch fun. The majority of the people doing dirty jobs, can't endure it without drugs, otherwise they accelerate their early graves; even though the substance itself (and its side-effects) have many harmful effects.

There are so many other reasons, which make people use hard drugs. Specifically it is used in order to kill the spirit of shyness, especially during those things done publicly and that is when you can control it. It can also help them face physical oppositions with some challenges either on physical combat or sissy. No one would want to go down with any embarrassment from anybody.

Any Freedom that doesn't Involve Jesus can't Last

Such elements have trained themselves to the extent they've become soft and gentle to the core on the look. It stimulates over gentleness and softness in human nature by taking it. That of course could later be a disadvantage to whom wanted to extract benefit from it on the other way round. They are easily forgiving people of their offences against them. It is a black business so many percentage of human races are into it; due to the quick financial income, which it yields to the business agents.

Anybody apprehended because of their involvement in drug trafficking is recorded a criminal by law. They go as far as choosing this in the spiritual realm, which might be relatively difficult for any adviser to just wake up with the intension of delivering anyone into this system of living. He or she is deeply rooted for quite sometime; you don't even know when, unless you're told.

Nothing exists without a foundation. And so, the kind of situation needed to be addressed from its foundation — with the word of God and prayer — by faith can help. Any freedom that does not involve Jesus can't last. Any deliverance that does not involve Jesus is fake and whomever that has obtain it cannot enjoy it.

Be informed, beforehand the foundation was laid. They laid the foundation in the kingdom of darkness with a price which is either by blood or something else, and may likely be so very precious to their lives. This is where so many people make mistakes that want to be like their neighbours at all costs.

Let's digress a bit. For example it's like when you see your co-traders inflate prices on their goods and yet people don't stop patronising them — even at such high prices — and it doesn't even affect their rate of turn-over. So you too would want to do the same thing, because you wouldn't want to be left behind.

Drugs are a Destroyer

Little did you know however, that their money was being programmed from the spiritual realm and so, however they may operate their business, it doesn't really matter any more. Some of them actually have no choice other than to accept this as their profession. When it has assess to a united family, it scatters it with chaos so that atrocities, malice and disunity become the order of the day, within a short period of time.

Cocaine is a locust, in that it has an evil spirit which controls it, that actually enhances its harmful impacts and the great damage it does to the bodies of those who take it. Don't you ever wonder, how come the money made from drug pushing usually fights a lot of battles to survive, for the naughty business fellow?

A man once told me that drugs are a destroyer. And that it had destroyed his home and even marriage. Someone may not know this but although it might be a quick source of cash generation and wealth, the consequences involved are a disaster all together. Many drug addicts have lost their lives to that substance. It is a dangerous product, which one is advised not to joke with.

A drug dealer is a criminal, both spiritually and physically. It is a true saying that even though you may succeed in running a drug business without being jailed for years (with the help of charm), still spiritually you must go. Their partners are not faithful, this is what everybody knows is a true saying.

Many Relationships have been Lost to Drugs

Even on normal grounds, when he is not being arrested, if the fiancée or wife is errand to deliver a quantity of substance to a customer and at the moment of exchange — see a law enforcement agent — pretend to be spouses and begin romancing each other, which some day might be tempted to taste it; mostly when the lady is morally loose. Many as a result of this have lost their relationships to drugs, even marriages.

If you are a smoker or you snort hard drugs or cocaine and your blood doesn't accept it — you must stop — else your attempts to proceed further, make you risk insanity. And you are bound to develop some strange behaviours, which may likely be abnormal and if care is not taken could result to madness. When it happens, out of shyness, some victims find it very difficult to explain their incidence and thereby prolong their cure. This is due to the impact it has on their thinking. Apart from the bargain, he or she had with demons, they also pay the devil as they progress with it, else the devil takes it by himself.

Even Worse than a Ravaging Disease

Through lawyers, bribing police, buying fake currencies and more, these activities accrue demons with vast resources. But even money gained legally (accumulated over years via proper means), can be flushed down the drain within a very short period of time due to addiction. It's like a disease that destroys so very rapidly. Cocaine is even worse than a ravaging disease, in so many ways. If it were possible to resurrect those who died from cocaine, they would speak their minds to this effect. I do believe someone is going to resign to renounce.

The devil at times looks at you and then works on your weak-points, on the basis of hard drugs, when he sees it is in you and that you are positive, he releases his arrow. Before now, he must have accessed it against your resources and social class in order to know if it can affect one or two things, whenever he decides to draw the rope of punishment or not.

So, you see that extravagantly, you are losing and secondly even politically your success is not a guarantee any more. Really, it is what you got the power to do in most cases that the assailants use in tempting you for a fall to a destruction. May the Lord God protect someone in Jesus' name. Life is a whole lot of battle; be informed. And may we be wiser than our enemies.

❖

Chapter 31

Love of Accidents

Fraud

Accidents are a thing that no rational being would want to happen, because they're deadly. It is a colliding of two or more movable vehicles, which in most cases can result in disaster; even the loss of life. Some lazy people who just do not care about the consequences, would love to be involved due to some benefits, which they feel can put them in a certain level of financial outreach.

In certain parts of the world, insurance is an obligation. Meaning, all vehicles are expected to have insurance contracts, each called premium with the insurance company. This is a guarantee to every vehicle moving or using the highway. In case of any emergency, the insurance of the vehicle at fault will help the second party to repair or buy his or her vehicle for peace.

Secondly, insurance companies are also responsible for the payment of the hospital bills, if the person is injured severely. The channels of the rules of the road users, go like this: car — motorcycle — bicycle — pedestrian. Since cars respect motorcycles; motorcycles respect bicycles and finally bicycles respect pedestrians.

So, due to this right order, some people take it as an opportunity to dabble into the highway, simply because they know if a car hits them, they are likely to receive one or two benefits as a compensation for the damages.

They also regard it as an opportunity to relax or rest and enjoy a salary not worked for. Apart from that, they also take it as a moment to catch fun and pleasure in their lives. They forget if peradventure they could not survive the accident, then, even the insurance benefit, they still cannot enjoy except their next of kin.

Life is Worth much more than Silver or Gold

Life is worth much more than silver and gold or even property, no matter what. Please, I suggest one shun such a dramatic system of living like a parasite. Deliberately, some will know quite well they will die if they engage, yet, they will still engage in the risk. Due to the self encouragement about the benefit the motive induces to their mind ahead and prompt the motivation to doing it. Maybe because they have life insurance, which they knew must have accumulated to some huge sum that the money can be paid to their families.

People Respect Money more than Life

Why all this? It is because in the first place, we all did not buy life we are using freely; hence, it is valueless to us. We seem to actually take it for granted. People respect money more than life, even human beings, as a whole entity.

And so, a family is respected and valued by what it's able to gather. For this reason, they want to pay for such a sacrifice, in order to bring about the availability of what is being yearned for within the family. But remember, whom you're deceiving is another human being just like you, even if he or she can't detect it in the prospect; your Creator sees all of you day in and day out.

Take care because the end shall tell about our dealings with one another. God simply knows those that care about the welfare of others and those that do not care.

CHAPTER 32

Love of Murderer

The Shedding of Human Blood

Murderers are people who deliberately like to take the life of their fellow human beings. Some intentionally like it because they feel it will definitely favour them as a secret method to carry out their evil mission of shedding the blood of their fellow human beings, for Satan. Through different means, Satan succeeded in using certain personalities to wreak havoc on their fellow human beings, on the basis of ritualism.

What he does first of all is to give them interest in occult practices, since the devil would need blood. Therefore, as he cannot do it for himself someone must do it for him. And so he will provide such a concerned body with the process, method and manner in which it can be carefully carried out and if possible will hide the truth of the whole mission.

The devil disrupts society with his delegated agents and uses blood to conduct his rituals. There's also the situation whereby in the act of self defence, the targeted victim, ends up killing the opponent. It can also happen in reaction.

Death that comes by the Tongue

Murdering goes beyond the ordinary use of man-made weapons of destruction. The tongue can kill through such things as: scandal, libel (defamation), allegations, false accusations and blackmail. The victims of such activity can be mutilated to the very marrow of their bones; to the point of committing suicide.

Be careful how you treat your fellow human beings, for life is fragile. A co-worker or colleague can cause fellow colleagues unemployment in this regard. People are facing a lot of challenges in their various working places. Don't be surprised if a co-worker doesn't need your fixed contract or promotion. This fellow you chat with every now and then because you work at the same company.

During your break-times you would sit together on most days and discuss life. Yet inwardly, he or she is harbouring something else in mind against you. You just can't predict human beings. None of your parents are directors of the company, so I don't see any reason why you should be against one another in your work place; the grudges are uncalled for. Therefore, pray to God in order to rubbish their mission even before they make you valueless in the office.

False Accusation

Lies can scare people away from their victims in order to deny them help from their helpers. For example, Geoffrey had promised to help David with a job, yet behold just two days before the appointment, it was alleged that David had murdered someone. This took the benefactor some time to verify, in order to know whether such allegations were true.

Why the verification? Because, a good name is better than great riches. Taking a murderer for a job vacancy will make you share a part of their record, even when the matter is still under investigation.

Beforehand, you were trusted with certain qualifications. After which it's your duty to protect your reputation and integrity and retain your ground in the company. If you slack, someone else may strive for your position. And if you allow them with some concrete evidence to nail you down oh, what a life? What a cataclysmic finish!

A murderer can also put on a fierce look, (opposite of the innocent face usually used to avoid being tagged or plainly recognised) . It is only evil that needs darkness as a garment for a coverage.

Sometimes, the appearance of someone can look very plainly hostile, maybe because he or she has killed his fellow human beings and so the vengeance of blood being shed is now at work. Due to that the fellow is not settled any more. Such a thing can make one suffer mental disarray and always become temperamental.

An unforgiving attitude is fast developed in them due to sissy. The ability to cope with fellow human beings and being normal is no longer there. They just can't confess such a heinous crimes, else they go to jail and nobody actually knows what is wrong with them; being in dilemma, they can't afford to let go with offences as it may look coward of them. Besides, it's common with the human phenomenon that nobody wants to be humiliated.

Offences

There are some who are cursed by it and so anytime they're offended with just a little misunderstanding, automatically to them such offenders are animals that need to feel the sharpness of their cutlass or even the demonstration of a gun or some other weapon.

Agents of Satan can extend the years of any projected mission by the killing their fellow human beings. It is piteous of any person to use their fellow human beings, as an egg of sanctification. It is very hard for a common man with the knowledge of God to believe such an intelligent ritualism is going on with men. They could project an accident to kill the targeted person in question as they don't want to be directly responsible for his or her mysterious death overnight.

King Saul tried it with David but it didn't work because God was with him and most importantly His word said: "Touch not my anointed and do my prophets no harm," (Ps 105:15).

All Bloodshed is a Ritual

Certain traditional demands could as well come up, which warrant that a fellow should be killed or put to death as the cultural law demands. An abominable act, which brings omens, calamity and bad luck to the land, can make the king or queen of the land to order them beheaded, for peace to reign.

Jehu killed Jezebel due to her fornications, which were reported to derail the entire economy of Israel as a nation (2 Kgs 9:22). Any act of shedding blood, which contains life, is a complete ritual.

❖

CHAPTER 33

Love of Disclosing Matrimonial Secrets

Avoiding Unnecessary Interferences

Anything concerning marriages should be kept secret from any third party in order to avoid unnecessary interference. There are so many half married women. You get to know them when they are doing something and secondly, the way they usually talk. Satan can easily overthrow them through his agents. The great problem is that the majority of them are not aware of this simple fact.

For example, their fellow women could just simply pose them with some questions. My sister how is your family or how are you coping with the family? The foolish woman will just reply thus: *"You know that useless good for nothing man. He has started again."* She never knew you were married to an idiot. You know what? You failed to have answered like that.

Recognise your Galloping Zone

The fact that the situation is hard on you at present does not mean you are going to remain like that forever. It could be your gallop now to your matrimonial vehicle on her journey to a greater height. You could be travelling across your galloping zone on your road of destiny, which means you are not going to remain there forever.

No condition is permanent, as they say. The storm must be over in some days, believe me. No condition is permanent. After all, the devil does not like happiness and so, he is glad when he hears of that. But I wish you knew instantly of what you derail yourself. Otherwise you would turn up a new live.

Similarly, some wrong or bad advisers can mislead you with wrong advice just to have you divorce your husband; whereas, she herself may have none. Every divorcee or bad single, would want that even her close married friend should come down to the same level with her. You may never know nor will it ever occur to you, in order to take caution, until you totally fall to become the same, with whomever is on this mission against you.

Bad Acquaintances are Alluring

A bad acquaintance can lure you into keeping extra-marital affairs. And if your husband does not like it, you are fired. Remember we all have culture; if you are not a Christian yet. And if you are a Christian you know the implications.

The cultural heritage was even reported to be enacted from the constitution of the Lord God. Due to the fact that our patriarchs are not Christians, they find it actually difficult to practice it so very perfectly well. That not withstanding, they both have punishment to render to any concerned body with a violation. You have heard of calamities and consequences; this is one of the things that births them.

Women who Soliloquise

Women that are so very flexible in this regard are those that marry to wealth. When money is going down, they begin to soliloquise and start narrating themselves to anybody who opens their teeth to them; and they open up to almost everyone. Why? In case, they are falling, so that they will immediately see who will receive or accept them very closely.

They thought it was very easy. Look, someone could be very fast and curious to hearing your story but lack with the interest to render you with any help. I do not know whether they want people to start envying them or not why they do it. Before they realise it, they will have succeeded in beckoning enemies into their homes, to come and dine with them because of the over-enjoyment of afternoon shadows.

In the olden days, no lady or woman told how her husband (man or boyfriend) makes love to her, but today they will discuss it and even describe how the man's private looks and how it goes in the door and comes out, to their friends. Why? For goodness sake. Many have thereby tempted their so called friends to go and try their loose husbands, in order to confirm the theory of what they were told, with practical effect. And when they are caught it is a complete disaster.

Why should a woman bombard her fellow woman with info so highly exaggerated in such away that will trigger her to think that her husband's private is nothing compared to her friend's husband. In some cases, women are like children who believe in giving whatever you tell them a try, in order to be very sure it is real (rather than ruminating over and over on theory, which in most cases is completely baseless).

Tell me your Friends and I will tell you who you Are

Too much conversation on telephones and the internet, (including any other form of communication), mean that some married women are victimised. The wise ones, do not stay too long on phones and are very mindful of their words during conversations. They must be faster than their friends; no matter what. Tell me your friends and I will tell you who you are. You and someone have been friends for quite sometime and so, you should be able to tell a little of her weak-points.

When she is about to go to that zone, you must be prepared what to say in order to counterbalance her intentions; the content of which is a total destruction (else you are a victim already). Anybody could be the serpent, which is so very subtle on a mission to destroying matrimonies; knowingly or unknowingly.

You that are the targeted must be wise in order to outsmart the snake with its evil mission. Be wise, snakes are still destroying homes until tomorrow. If you don't want to cry, losing your marriage, wage war against it with all tactics in the name of Jesus. Don't say I didn't warn you.

The devil saw that there was excellence in human beings. He saw that if he was not a part of it, he would lose too much. *"If I'm not a part of this splendid, it can never be. It is better to be scattered in all ramifications, than for me not to be part of the glory that humans render to God,"* the devil considered. *"It is going to be so very much awesome indeed. I can't just sit back and let it be."*

Glory

"Because in heaven all angels are praising only one God. And on the earth again God is still saying go and multiply (Gn 1:28) and really all the people on earth will be praising Him in the prospect, after all said and done. No, this is going to be too much. I must attack human beings such that they cannot comply with God. And as such God cannot have the whole glory as supposed. That verse, was just the summary of everything about human nature and their appointments by God to man – God's glory."

Today, isn't Satan using those who've danced to his tune in the mission of disrupting peace and tranquillity in churches, in public gatherings, in schools, in organisations, in homes, offices, in companies, in leadership and many more? Of course, yes. They are on the mission that if their master the devil is not going to be part of the enjoyment then it should not hold. The glory thereof must be divided or else no way.

This is why the Christians are strongly praying every now and then against these uninvited elements or neighbours who are out there ready to cause problems for those peaceful people in our human society and churches of Jesus Christ.

If not, God only made mankind for His praise and worship; the strong prayers we all pray as believers are as a result of that. May the good God deliver us. Only God knows who is really who (Rv 2:9).

❖

CHAPTER 34

Love of Complaining

Individual Preferences

Nobody, whether individuals, family, clan, quarter, street, company, group, nation or government, are complaining without something worrying them. As everyone needs freedom over one problem or the other, if reverse is the case of his or her expectation, it results in nothing except complaints. And consider those who are one hundred years old, they too still like wealth, even if they've only got a few years to enjoy that wealth (at least they can leave something behind for their children to enjoy after them).

Others complain of sickness and the lack of money to buy tablets. Pains shorten our joy, which also makes us complain even more, (especially around those who possibly have a solution to our problems!)

Then there's individual preferences, for example, we prefer one particular climate for another. Like the Africans who have tasted some European countries with snow and cold or scarcely not. And so, someone who has tasted can as well tell the difference between both. While the Europeans like the cold weather more than the hot weather.

Worry Instigates Complaining

God expects everyone to reproduce in (Gn 1:28). But sometimes, you feel worried over being a single, because you have attained the age to settle down with someone and raise a family. A very many will settle down and begin to battle with barrenness. Children are results of marriage. And if it is not forth coming even when due, the concerned person becomes worried. If at the process of searching for a life partner, you mistakenly join with the wrong one, you are finished. If two of you are not in mutuality, such failure in parental responsibility can make you complain to a third party.

If a student finds a particular subject in his scope so very difficult, it can pose them with running helter-skelter in search for a more intelligent student or teacher to put them through. In order not to fail exams, he or she must read well, in order to enhance knowledge acquisition as soon as possible. Inability to meet up with school-fees is another very big problem, which poses the threat of being in disarray, if care is not taken.

A political appointee or a candidate whose campaign does not yield positively is bound to worry over the huge sum of money spent during the election process. If a person cannot sense any sign of it being lucrative, then he sobers and wonders why the stagnancy? The purpose for setting up a good business is for profit. Therefore, if he or she is not realising any gains (or running at a loss), then they contemplate whether to change the business or stop it altogether.

Complain to God for Help

If you gain employment as an employee, you are expected to possess the required skill rightly needed for the job. And if you know within yourself that you are not quite meeting up with the required standard of the company, then you must complain to God, for help.

Almost everybody wants to possess extravagant assets and other material acquisitions. If the reverse is the case, where you don't have what others have or what you actually want to have, then you are envious, jealous and complain.

You wish to travel around the world, which of course would cost a huge sum of money. Therefore, if you can't meet up with the means of doing so, you complain and worry. When we pray to God, we expect answers but if it is not forth coming, we are shaken in our faith.

So many people are afraid to live their lives comfortably in their homes due to how they are always harassed and attacked by criminals. And that is to tell you that there are people actually living dramatic lives.

Sometimes, it is destined. You never can tell since destiny travels without listening to anybody. Racial discrimination and racisms are part of apathy against humanity and it is everywhere. The back-races complain that the white-races don't smile at them, while the whites are also saying something concerning black-pride.

The Brotherhood of Nature

Do you know something, you aren't actually the one doing this complaining, but it's your blood, of the brotherhood of nature. And that error needed to be corrected, over a perversion of many years a go.

How can elder be forced to serve even the younger. The fact that you are productive doesn't make you the elder. The fact that you are so very advanced technologically doesn't really make you the elder. Shem — father to the Asians is the eldest brother, followed by Ham — father to the Africans and of course Japheth — father to the Europeans the youngest. Whether or not you like it, things are falling to normal in the sense, truth is about to prevail. The Asians will soon provide a nation that will serve as a world power while the Africans will not remain the slaves forever.

Blood of nature is agitating can't you see! Open your eyes. Don't let the technological advancement blindfold your intelligence, by nature. We shall all know the truth and the truth will set us all free and we all shall enjoy it (John 8:32). Due to these barriers, integration is completely lagging for now. However, men and women, youth and children, you are not the ones doing all these expressions that you are making; rather truth and justice are striving to prevail. It will soon be in Jesus' name. God blesses you.

Stay Tuned...

Stay tuned, options will definitely satisfy you. You could be living in the same building, working in the same company, shopping in the same supermarket/boutique, using the same road, yet your dealings toward one another will be like two completely parallel lines. Let heaven and earth contract; the intimate relationship is still not far above, (give or take levels) hence there is still a bridge. Don't worry, very soon the head shall no longer deny the hair of its position.

America looks like a nation, in fact every global collective nationality came together and formed, in order to make a nation. Don't let technology deceive you, which has given her the position she is in today. In reality, only nature will prove this dangerous truth, which lies in here. But I do believe very soon it will manifest for us all to see and witness. And I believe also that it will not just be the balance equation will benefit everybody. Truth is the answer.

❖

CHAPTER 35

Love of Hair

A Form of Identification

Hair is the beauty of a woman and a symbol, which is a total identification of her womanhood. It is also a symbol when looking at her from afar that whispers to your mind, *"Look, this person is a woman."* The hair could be either long, short or average. The long hair gives a woman much fit than the short or even average. Out of fashion is what gives rise to short and average hair. Another cause of it is if wrong hair-cream is applied, hair can also become short. That was natural.

Artificially, some people can also decide to cut their hair short due to imitation of its reigning-styles. Weavons and attachments can also make the difference.

Some ladies of nowadays are fond of colouring their hair for fashion reasons. This normally happens for different reasons and on different occasions. Maybe the outfit suitable for that occasion required a kind of hairstyle that worked best with a coloured weavon. Some men and women are very interested in attractive hairstyles, which give them a different figure among others on special occasions.

Most men also dye their hair, especially the side close to their foreheads (just a little), which is either white or any other attractive sharp colour to match appropriate attires, which suit. The style of hair a man cuts can determine what the face will reflect at a glance, at the end of the day.

Cultural Choices

Culturally, people make all types of hairstyles that best represent their acclaims, which could either be their juju, fraternity, religion or other. But as a child of God, you must know the type of hairstyle that your Lord and Saviour will gain the most glory from, and will also rain blessing on you. When the glory goes up, blessings come down. God has purchased us with the blood of Jesus.

This is a distinctive bargain in the sense, He is not going to resell us as with the case of a business transaction. In business, anything you purchase means that you are going to resell for profit, in order to generate more income. But the only profit here I think we all are going to yield God is the glory thereof; nothing else. Therefore, as we are living, we are no more living for ourselves rather living for God (2 Cor 5:15).

Many have received their indirect initiations into the demonic kingdom, unknowingly due to hairstyle. May the good God deliver us. This is why you must desist from living your lives by fashion. Be yourself just as you are made by your Creator not as you imitate your neighbour, else your lives cannot give glory to God. You are a special person distinctively different from every other person.

Besides, individuals have special treasures within them, which the secret codes lie in between him or her with God. And so, for your destiny or life to yield God with praise, without any reproach, you must strive to maintain your integrity in order to retain your ground in Him.

❖

CHAPTER 36

Love of Outfit or Dressing

Body Advertisement

Dressing is good. You dress in order to look very decent to yourself and to the eyes of onlookers, to the glory of God. You dress to look good. This we know attracts certain respect, based on human culture, even in our modern era. It qualifies your identity, since humanly we normally consider the appearance of any fellow. Due to this advantage, some ladies embark on making certain fabric with stylists, which help to speak for them as regard body advertisement. A lady's outfit can connect her with a man, either for dating, a relationship or even for marriage.

Men are not left out from this point. As girls also like to take a second glance at guys because they are well dressed.

However, the idea of dressing and appearance go beyond mere relationships and marriage. It can induce a contract, a job, business connection, even with someone that matters very much to you.

Clothes can make you have a name, which does not suit you. How? Because something that is supposed to credit you, can instead discredit you. For example, the majority of our single ladies don't have a single thought about going around wearing clothes that accentuate the shape of their bodies, due to fashion. (Similarly, some dress and begin to display swagging movements in order to get male customers).

To Gain Attraction

They are just busy working mechanically to gain attraction but forget that they have high-heels on (or other unsuitable footwear). High-heel shoes can be disappointing at times, due to certain paths that you may be trekking. I would advise you to dress simply, with the right outfit, which is suitable for the right occasion.

Looking at a guy with the corner of your eye could get you attracted to him. Who on earth that does not like good thing? Absolutely, nobody. Therefore, she who wants the best (if her faith is based on outfits) should as well learn to dress and look decent.

There should be times that one dresses with mixed colours. A casual dress, shoes for walking and elegant sandals for outfits. Let it at least match your clothes. This is because many are still very much ignorant in this. To wear a suit, a tie with sport shoes is totally off fashion and unconscious. I suggest that if you put on the opposite of what is required for the right occasion, don't even bother to come out.

Step out with Class and Style

It's a good friend who tells you the faults of your poor outfit choices; while others will only whisper and ridicule you behind your back. Always step out with class and style even though it could be as little as you can afford. Make sure it is in line with the proper way of dressing.

Your dressing should be such that it's catching, which is capable of keeping your right guy waiting. If you are both setting for a special occasion, your being involved should crown it all. Please, dress according to your class. Situations where a married woman dressing like a single girl or a girl dressing like even a married woman is thought provoking. It can induce embarrassment on the women and prevent them connecting with the right guys for marriage.

To be dressed correctly is vital for mature ladies; it helps to accelerate their marriage and secures them against any kind of embarrassment and gives them the respect they deserve.

A particular dress code can introduce a prostitute, a divorcee, and even a lady that is lippy. Some persons are very good at reading this. The issue of judging someone by appearance does reflect at times so very correctly. It is sometimes applicable. It makes you to know every careering woman: a mother in short.

Following the Seasons

Clothes have the correct time and season to wear them. That takes us to seasons. So, carefully following them determines the type of clothes you put on at a particular point in time. For example we have summer and winter. In summer, the fabric which is cotton is suitable for the heat and breeze; with necessary jewellery such clothes should not be too clingy nor too boggles.

For example, tiny bodies with big bottoms or wide waists, should be able to know their size of clothes. But it should be fitting according to your shape. Winter fluctuates style and suitable fabrics for the time, like jackets, tops, trousers, tight-gloves, caps, with some simple appropriate jewellery and wristwatches. Followed by feast clothes like Christmas and New-year.

These two consecutive feasts stimulate much interest and focus on fashion; depending on the race and culture of an individual. Remember this period is very unique that as a man or woman, some cash must be left in the purse or wallet. If you must completely feel the importance of the feast. Men are mostly about the shoes, belts, wristwatches, shorts and trousers. In most cases, shoes dictate the occasion: office, sport, casual and occasional shoes.

Traditionally, cultural fabrics are noted among the African race. You can't beat an African woman for this; most especially the Western part of Africa. They have coloured the Western designer green. Cotton, lace and more, suit African tropical weather. The skirt and blouse are simply made such that they are trending. The old and the young people love it in Africa. Everyone makes it to suit his or her shape and style and as well as the right fabric. It is noted as the traditional attire for the Africans wherever they are in the world.

Knowing your Body Type

Finally, there is a type of clothing that we have not discussed yet, known as jeans, which are for everybody. Already made and available in every size for every person on the earth. There are different types such as: baggy, leggy, thin, pencil, three-quarter and low-waist jeans. So, everyone should know the type that suits them best, for every occasion. Be aware that too tight jeans could pronounce your thigh either too tinny or too fat; preferably stretching is good.

Know your body type and shape, this is what matters most, not what is in vogue. This is because some people horribly run and buy what is reigning without minding the fitting and colour, which suit them. Rounded or curving shapes are not the same as medium or large size busts. And again, thick waists with small bottom and tinny or small legs give another different posture in dressing. You cannot compare flat-boot, straight legs, v-boot with big breast etc.

Ladies shoes with corresponding bags match. Then there's dressing to kill. Armies going to war, of course do not tie wrapper, otherwise it is no longer a warring outing, rather cultural attire for something else. There is that of a native doctor, which could symbolise danger or other. There is farm clothing, which of course makes people identify what you are out for. Going fishing also has clothing properly designed for it. Then to pray in shrines, the concerned priests must have particular types of clothing, that he wears for his ministry on behalf of the people; without which he can't approach the juju.

In Exodus, there were specific clothes specially designed for the priests to minister in the house of God. Aaron and the two sons were examples of this illustration about clothes, confirmed in Exodus 28:1.

❖

CHAPTER 37

Love of Communication

The Sharing of Ideas

This is an act of having a chat with any person. For example, animals of the same or different species communicate. Communication can be oral, even in sign or by using symbols, to express one's feelings to another at any particular point in time. One can only share ideas through communication. It does so much to the body, which is either good or bad. Through communication, you can credit and gratify someone over a job well done. As the saying goes; a problem shared, is half solved. It can help relieve grief and pains.

Communication helps you to know the depth of the mind of someone towards you. From the abundance of the heart a man speaks (Mt 12:34, Ps 14:1). It can add or reduce one's dignity and personality. Blackmail and blasphemy come through communication.

Evil communication they say can corrupt good manners (1 Cor 15:33). It serves as business to those who are full of freedom against their neighbours. You can only request for any through communication. And that is the only source by which one can make one's problem known to whom is directly have a solution for it. No one has seen God face to face. Asking Him for a blessing is done by communicating with Him in prayers.

One of the things that can limit or restrict our communication is simple mouth odour. When your mouth smells so badly, whatever you say doesn't matter; nobody wants to listen or cares whether you're right or wrong.

Flowing with the People around You

Mouth odour can be due to infection or something else. Something ordinary can cause it or a spiritual attack by powers trying to cage your ability from flowing with the people around you. If you find out that it's an internal disease, I suggest you go for a check-up; which is either by your private doctor or direct with the hospital.

Everybody has his or her own problems. Your problem may or may not be mouth odour. Another person's could be body odour, but in an attempt to resolving the situation, you discover that shyness is another problem of its own to tackle.

Shyness is a Barrier

Shyness is a barrier. If you don't know how to deal with it, you just can't relate your problem with anybody who might even be a solution to it. A lot of personalities have been denied solutions to their problems, based on uncontrollable ego that they tend to put on before even their messiahs.

Some may not even be able to express their feelings quite well to the understanding of the listeners and as such will not be able to receive their expected answers to their situations. Some who are into problems, at times may not have the faith and interest, that whom they want to approach got the real solution needed for their problem.

If you are into any bargain with anyone and it happens you lack communication as a medium of exchange of feelings with the latest info about the movement, problem can set in. Communication is a medium by which we all talk to our Creator. It's important that you know it's the same with man and animal alike. And so, keep it up, a solution lies in there. Some day it will emerge; God blesses you.

❖

CHAPTER 38

Love of Freedom

Freedom of Expression

Freedom is the right to do every good thing. It is the right to enjoy every good thing you wish to have and enjoy. It is the right to freedom of expression and even of one's opinion. It is the right to also make a speech. It is the right to individual movement. It is a freedom of worship etc. Anybody can therefore, decide as to which religion he or she is to belong or not without external interference. It goes beyond just this ordinary context in the sense, everybody needs it from the great to the least, in every nation, even as far as the government.

No nation will be glad to have a ravaging disease like HIV/AIDS as an epidemic or pestilence just as parts of the world experienced in 2019/20. This is the period the whole world experienced a global trend, which made both the criminal and non criminal agents to remain completely indoors, as though it were a total house arrest.

Even the unbelievers got to realise that there is God. And that freedom matters; most importantly, thanks be to God who had given us freedom to consume freely without any demand of payment.

Individuals and governments had their pains throughout. The economy was rusticated down below even the already alarming global economic crises. On all accounts, purses and wallets were reduced of a certain percentage of income. The governments purposely demanded for charity from some well-to-do individuals, personalities, companies, banks got their supposed yearly dividends confiscated for this. Educational systems were totally disorganised in the sense, the students were restricted to learning through the internet, which has never been in the history of mankind. Many souls went down like fowls killed by fowl disease.

Optimum Equilibrium

Individuals and government have different pains. Fear griped the mind of many to the extent, it was reported that the German Prime Minister committed suicide. It could be so very different such as: sickness, penury, business and economic flop. And so, it will be a thing of joy to such a nation if it can attain her state of optimum equilibrium in both business and economy, security of life and property, which automatically will affect the people and government for good. Covid19 will be a thing everyone will live to remember; I tell you such a quarantine was so horrible. It was a trend in short.

A student would want a state of freedom from failure and lack of knowledge, which concerns their scope of study. Every student wants freedom from academic stress. Rational couples do not want any atom of disunity in their matrimonial union-hood or in their homes. Children would want to enjoy the best from their parents. If you ask any child what he or she would want from their biological parents, you find out that the list is endless.

Teachers and lecturers in various institutions, both government's and private's would want students to easily comprehend their teachings once and for all. Except the demonic ones who do not want the progress for the students and others.

Freedom to Succeed

The technologists want to always advance in their inventions everyday. Transportation wants to be able to contribute a greater percentage of a good quota to economic record of its nation. Every geographical area of any given land inhibited by people will want ideal security. Some elements prefer to die than to be poor. Some said they just can't afford to be paupers. While others said: "Get rich or die trying."

Friends do not want division in their midst. Patients want freedom of sickness. Oh! If only they could stand to their feet again once more just to enjoy their free gift of nature: good health that money cannot buy. That's the foundation of all wealth, you can say that again. Someone wants to be able to breath freely and perfectly who has been breathing with difficulties. Everybody engages in one good thing or another and wants to be rich.

The Importance of Freedom

Freedom is very important. If you have it, you just don't need security. Even as the president of a nation, you can dress ordinarily just like every other common person on the street and stroll around just to know how people feel concern about your governance. You can only relate with the masses if you have provided the benefit already. You can't tell me that as a president of a nation, you neglected to provide for your people (and besides being conscience stricken) you still have the audacity to walk on the street, just like that. It's not possible. You will not even have the boldness to do that because to you everybody is a suspect.

In demand of freedom, somebody wants to be able to exchange clothes. Little babies want to be able to feed by themselves with little or not even assistance from anybody. The average person wants a state whereby they can collect money by themselves and be able to put it right in their pocket, without being cheated by others.

A celebrant of any occasion wants a state of silence without fight or any physical engagement about anything whatsoever related to two having lock-up heads and all that. Car drivers want every highway to be freed from hold-ups or traffic jams, even accidents. A smooth highway, no potholes, no barriers, no obstacles, no hindrances and so on, is the desire of the motorist using the roads every now and then.

No living being wants to die. But it's a pity that no amount of money can be paid to God, in order to live forever (Ps 49:7-9). If it were possible, the price would be so very expensive, that not a single person could afford it. And those who can't pay, that's the end. This means, you are not worthy to live. We all want to live happily all the time and would not want to hear anything, which will scatter our joy or happiness to be made mentioned among us. We all want love among mankind, if possible, to function everywhere.

The Love of God

Surprisingly even the ideal likeness we tend to practice towards one another, which is still conditional: (give or take the material and financial basis is lagging certain requirements due to imperfection, which set in at the beginning of human nature till now). I hereby refer someone to the story of the garden of Eden; to be concise and realistic and candid. Therefore, what you have to offer will determine the percentage of love any fellow will exercise on you.

Of all these, only the living God has the thorough love for both the good and the bad ones. His wish is that everyone should come to a genuine repentance (2 Pt 3:9). Such a change that destruction can no longer be before the person anymore; forever and ever again; though he or she may die physically but in the spirit, his soul will be alive again and live forever. Really, the Lord God would want everybody to change, in order to actually avert the damnation and the consequence of sins.

The legislators want a state whereby every citizen of their nations would be law abiding, even as far as the foetus in their mothers' wombs. The law enforcement agents do not want to undergo the stress it takes to make people obey the constitutions guiding the nations in which they operate. It is very hard to deal with human beings. And so also it is hard to get along with them.

Business people want to run their businesses successfully with confidence and more also with confiding and honest partners in the business for good. To be sure with a successful guarantee in the business, you need God, faithful and honest business partners/customers as any business person; without which no way because the world is humanly hard today. The contractors want their contracts to be numbered serially according to how they arrive to the extent of their numerous.

Bountiful Harvest

Farmers want to be able to harvest bountifully with minimum stress. The advanced ones want to be able to produce on a very large scale, in order to meet up with the public demand by a greater supply of his or her farm produces. Besides, he or she wants to enjoy government subsidies as a confiding farmer, on every necessary means by which his or her scope of production can be met like: machineries, fertiliser, irrigations and a very large piece of land for farming on a very large scale. There should be a provision of the means by which the farm produce can conveniently undergo a preservation for a long period of time, before being consumed. And this increases the nation of her food supply.

Who feeds well can hardly be sick. Individuals are immune by adequate feeding first of all; let alone with other ideal treatments. A farmer won't be happy by having their farm overgrown with grasses because the crops can't do well in such conditions. From pests eating up the crops, or from diseases destroying the crops and animals being effected by disease also.

Inability to farm on a very large scale is not at all the dream of any farmer, even the local traditional farmers. Everybody wants to gain, in whatever he or she does. I do mean, profit is the number one incentive/motive of every business, as far as results are concerned. And so, no one yearns for a loss. The wise are trying to live above foolishness. Important figures are trying to maintain their levels; just to avoid being disgraced and abashed.

Freedom from Bureaucracy & Mismanagement

Governments want freedom from bureaucracy. Leaders are praying for their instructions and orders to be adhered to by their subjects. Every person wants to be freed from lack of transportation; individually and publicly. Freedom is very important, if you have it, you don't even need security.

Governments cannot afford to have their nation soiled and ruined by irrelevant systems, such as nepotism.

Mismanagement is like a ravaging diseases generally fighting against the economic growth and development, of any nation. Any nation that has experienced fraud and bankruptcy with its central bank most especially risks long hardship/ crises. And such must pray for help from Almighty God, the final formula for a resolution. It is more or less square, as a relegation, which will force any victimised nation to embark on seeking for a loan from neighbouring countries. If you have enough to manage your affairs or resources, there is no need to borrow.

Above all, war, terrorism, flood and earthquakes, including epidemics, can induce nations with certain backwardness. So far so good, freedom from these is a very big blessing to the beneficiary nations. I repeat in a nut shell that company, group, individual, clan, quarter, street, community, local government, or zone, state, country or nation, continent, and even the whole world needs freedom in one way or the other for the sake of simplicity.

❖

CHAPTER 39

Love of Greeting

Reciprocal Respect

Respect they say is reciprocal. Greeting is very important to both young and old. It stimulates closeness. It is a natural practice, which always comes to sharing on an equal basis. You can't tell me that someone you always greet can still pose you with some difficulties by appearance to approach with your problems as to knowing if he or she can be of help to you.

It makes you social and defines your cultural heritage. It can ease your free conversation with people: above, bellow and even your equal or same class with you. Being influential through greeting can ease your help, which you may directly be in need of at a particular point in time.

Greeting can induce you with a good connection for a business and marriage. All kinds of blessings are also attached to respect. I know you could be respectful and some people would not like it. Keep it up; don't let them shatter it for you. It is not a sycophancy to the understanding, rather it is heading you towards a goal that matters.

The first sign you notice is a good name, which is more or less a preferable option to great riches. No matter the bad disgustful mouth by some irrelevant evil people, if you can undermine their negative reactions towards you and you are able to beat the gravity below any of your limitations to forge ahead, the sky is your limit. I bet you anything that one does very well is taking one to somewhere. It will come to a time that enemies to your greetings would want to make friendship with you because they now realise their fault.

Being Yourself

Everyone must not make it with the same way and type. Stick to your own and let's see what becomes of it in the nearest future. In other words, when you are not just discouraged of being yourself, success is smiling at your door very soon. Keep it up, everybody cannot be the same; no, never. May your mind grasp the understanding about greeting with the right motive to the glory of our Lord God. Very soon, option of the Lord's reward over goodness will satisfy you; definitely.

❖

CHAPTER 40

Love of Visitation

Showing Up

An act to decide to pay someone a visit outside one's immediate home of being, organisation, institution, hospital, for a private talk or others in order to express one's feelings towards the fellow to whom visit is paid or one or two other things. There are so many uncountable reasons for a visitation. One could decide to visit a medical doctor for an examination for one's body systems for a check- up/diagnose. A friend could still be in hospital either being sick of something for a visit by whomever as when due. On the other hand, she could put to birth, and so it's your duty to show up. But it must never be occasion to gossip.

Visitation does not just exist for nothing. It is either you practice it to show love to one another or to sound a serious warning over one or two things. So many bad people visit a place, family, bank, company, in order to access it and to know how to strategise to boggle in overnight or at day time in order to rob as the case maybe. The majority of ritualists are very lucrative in this system, where security is not so ideal.

Self Flattery & Intimidation

Really, the saying that all fingers are not equal is true in the sense, it is vividly noticed among groups of friends. Most guys and ladies are very frequent in their friend's places just because the other has not much money to buy clothes, therefore, visit to show up with clothes, in order to intimidate them.

The ladies also show up in jewellery, wristwatches, bangles, make-up and shoes etc. Like for example, you want to try me? Is their popular statements. You need to come to see how my dad, my mum or my guy: new catch/new fish is showering me with some money these days. Anyway, I just came to show you my car besides, they just imported some sets of creams for me and I am so confused; I just don't even know what to do; as to which to apply or wear first.

Replied, Clever, is that so? I am so happy for you. I cannot wait to see them. See my new cell phone in short. Oh! Wonder shall never end. I beg don't forget me. Even if it is the fragrance, let it diffuse to reaching me. Similarly, some ladies purposely nicer and short their skirts in order to show or display laps with shining skins to friends and people.

More also, they can mix the cream they use with oil in order to make their skins so very much shiny, reflective and even sparkly to the eyes, for attractions if possible by the concerned bodies as far as opposite sexes are concerned. So, if they can't speak, their skins will definitely do the speaking for them, to make you ask them questions about the secret of their sudden shining skins. From there, they start with self flattery. If you turn the ignition, the key must respond. You can understand.

One day, there was this guy whose elder brother just came from the United States of America. Do you know what? This guy just quickly took the brother's car for a car wash with the hope to drive it that same evening; probably as an opportunity to intimidate to luring even catch a girl for a love of bed overnight. Friends, guess what behold! He was but disappointed as at 10 p.m., the car in question was still not washed by the car washer.

Information & Gossip

Who comes to visit you often, and what does he or she come to do and what does he or she want? If I may say or come to the juncture, is either he or she comes to relate information or gossip. Or he or she has come in order to relate and re-relate just to fill in the gap of a mission as was assigned or errand against you. Visitation has so much embedded in it which both the host and the visitor are not left out of the result. Some use it to access their friends privacy; in order to know how he or she lives and as well as the material wealth he posses in their closets.

The time has come where seven ladies will purposely summon a guy or a man and say please, let us clothe ourselves up with the same attire and buy you a car, rent an apartment for you or even build you a home with the condition that you must accept to be called our husband; so that we will not have to go bearing the shame of not being married. The scripture says something regarding this in Isaiah 4:1.

Due to this dangerous fact, this era has embraced whereby girls or ladies visit their girlfriends in order to drag their guys/husbands with them. Some girls drag boyfriends with the fellow girlfriends. The same visit make many foolish guys to engage in dragging girlfriends even wives with their so called bosom friends.

Some people quarrel over children and with visit of either them or their delegates they can know how to embark on snatch the children from the present compound. Kidnappers also use this medium. Unfriendly friends can also use this method in order to poison the targeted personalities in question. Probably, he or she must have been paid for it or he decides to do it as self business, which is either for an intervention for a reaction as a mission or being sent by some other persons.

Jealousy can Emerge

You just can't access any home without visit it as to know its daily routines. Apart from that, you can also know your standard of living whether you are actually measuring up or you are below your standard and those that you are above and that are above you also. Eyes can never develop any act of cut-throat over what it has not seen. Jealousy can emerge at the sight of something during a visitation to any home.

Consolation & Condolence

Well, nobody is actually omniscience; knowing it all. And as such, one could decide to visit each other for a lesson, advice and others. Ministers in the vineyard of the living God have their days of counselling people about things or issues pertaining to their lives. Some elders are very good in giving a very good advice to those that are concerned for their future benefits. The words of our fathers are truly words of wisdom. You could visit a friend in school. Parents can decide to visit their child or friend from school in order to actually know whether the report about him or her is true or not.

Those whose freedoms are restricted, maybe because of their crimes committed as a result of which they have been jailed and then have their freedom in curtain. They would need visits for a consolation or else, they get frustrated and commit suicide.

Even the bereaved would need condolence, which necessitates a visitation. If visitation weren't necessary, Jesus wouldn't tell the disciples, thus: I was in prison you visited me (Mt 25:36). At the process of sorrow and grief over the lost of his loved one; you console him or her. Representatives to the Presidents do visit nations collectively; which they are warmly received and welcomed during which they have a hand shake with a stir of love to one another; but does it really cut to the base? I leave that question with you to answer.

❖

CHAPTER 41

Love of Shopping

To Keep Life Going

Is an act of buying or purchasing of any material goods, food and other things needed by man to effect a change in outfit as well as nourishment in order to keep life going. Shopping can be subdivided into casual food and clothes; commercial, fun and others. Casual: Everyone knows that food and clothes are part of the basic necessities of man.

As it is not possible for everybody to be self sufficient, therefore, there is every necessity that you must buy what you cannot produce from others that are in charge. You could call this a circular kind of services. Commercial: this is a via or process goods passed through from production centres to get to the final consumers.

Traders and all business persons are responsible in this category. Fun: almost everybody these days is interested in coming out beautiful and cutting even elegantly by looking just so very decent in dressing with a quality befitting outfit. We are talking about money anyway.

Matching the Required Standards

Girls of nowadays yearn for guys that always do a kind of surprise visit with presents, or some gifts and as well as taking them out for a shopping; these are those whom girls or ladies delight most. If a guy never appeared clean and good looking, no beautiful girl sees him as anybody. The same thing is applicable to ladies to guys that base their choices on outfit. In order to be able to match up with required standards of the modern era. And so, if you must catch a clean fish: guy or girl, you must be correct in latest fashions, as far as outfits are concerned.

That includes seeing, time and period to really give public your utmost best in: clothing, caps, eye-glasses, gloves if need be. Make sure you don't miss it because if you do, you may just be regarded as off and on guy or lady in the eyes of the viewers. Remember the mirror must be your close friend this time around; else, along the line, there could be error in the make-up. How? Well, you can hug some people who joke expensively and you have it tampered with and so correction must be made even before reaching your destination. It could as well shower a bit and I am sure you know what that means?

Apart from fun for enticement, one could still decide sometimes or some days to do away with dwelling perpetually on old clothes and shoes by changing one's wardrobe of clothes and shoes if possible, depreciated jewellery are not left out also. If your power or money attain, there is also a need if possible to change your car by trying to move along with the wind of the latest; that makes you in short, one of the biggest guys in town.

On Top of the World

I bet you if you are able to rise to match up with this standard you are on top of the world and I can imagine how many ladies would be crazing to be crush with you or even strive in order to crust just to identify with you. They will so flock you like no other. They always like to identify with a guy riding in one of the clean good looking machines — best of cars for as a means of his mobility; at least those she once played with will not just see her any how again now; simply because she has up graded. Besides, almost every lady believes in a guy riding in the best of cars to be the right man for a husband.

One thing is to be rich and another thing is to be able to maintain and control the wealth. This is because, many are a people who had clothes but has confused of how to wear, wash and maintain them. And this has made the public to abhor it on seeing it on their waist.

Dirty people are still very much whom they are, they can never be changed, it is not by new dress or changing of wardrobe every now and then that matters. They change furniture, electronics, DVDs movies, musical CDs, books and Biros, and then donate the old ones to charity homes for their generosity as an act to expressing their care for the destitute. Shops also require a stock-up to date occasionally in order to replace the already bought of all kinds of food items and goods.

❖

CHAPTER 42

Love of Colour of Any Object

Beautiful to Behold

Object could be anything abstract, concrete or solid, animate or inanimate. Normally, colour is awesome and beautiful to behold. Similarly, man made objects can be sprayed or painted in order to suit its desirable beauty the owner would want of it. It could be house or one other things; they all carry their different colours respectively. That is why all objects and houses bearing different colours as: white, yellow, black, brown, red, purple, blue, green etc.

Humanly, we have even the black, white, yellow, chocolate, red, Caucasian among human race. Even though we all have different skin colours respectively but we all use the same common noun blood; though different in DNA also, which contents must relatively differ from what flows in our veins. This also extends to their colour of hair respectively. Colour of hair actually varies. We have black-hair, which could be either strong, hard or soft.

This is commonly found among every race in the world. White-hair is found among the white race similarly, some of them also grow golden and red hair. In black race, we have albinos, whose hair is red only. Generally, white-hair can only be grown on somebody's head when he or she is growing older; or artificially coloured. This has no exception nor either select race.

Colourful Hair Dyes

Artificially, some elements dye their hair in order to bring their desirable colour, which could be either to retard grey-hair, which might be growing already. Secondly, fashion can make someone to dye his or her hair in order to give him another colour like: yellow, black, red, white, blue, green, name them; depends on what the person directly wants. Everybody prefers one colour to the other.

This is why we do not wear the same colour of clothes. We do not drive the same colour of car. We do not build the same pattern of house nor paint with the same colour either. We do not possess the same furniture in our houses or offices even companies. We don't wear the same shoes and sandals on our legs. We all have different electronics in our houses and what have you. Some ladies would prefer red make-up kit, white costume etc.

In revelations or dreams, it is also noticed that colour could either be a symbol of blessing or of a danger. For example, red colour in the dream signifies love but however, only God knows whether it is genuine or fake love at the end. In the road traffic, the red light means stop to the road users whether vehicles or pedestrians. It is a total offence to beat it, even risk fines with the government by the law enforcement agents.

When you disobey the government, you disobey God that put her in that leadership position. For no authority that exist apart from the one ordained by God (Rom 13:1). It is a complete rebel to rival with the positive authority. God does not hold the operators guiltless. Even when authority is negative, you can only speak the truth to her ears and thereby leave her with God.

Love of Appearance

Everybody likes new things, except due to scarcity of resources to have it when it is reigning. It is a part of fun as one of the bests one would expect. Nobody wants to be counted last in our society; instead we all want first class. It makes you show up just like every others in due season and time. It could as well introduce you a wealthy person before others. Your outfit can even add colours to your appearance and thereby make you even look very decent.

In the Western world, due to various laws, the majority are on advantage in the sense, they change like people actually changing clothes on their waists. The question is, how do they do it? They simply take their old cars to a dealer in order to value it and then add money to carry or even buy another one.

Sometimes, you find out that, it necessitates that you get some old clothes in order to sustain or preserve the new ones to last long. And so, in that case, getting some used clothes for yourself doesn't make you a complete poor person. Income, we all know does determine a demand. Contact must come to a time whereby you have to buy used clothes and amend them to your taste in order to balance up yourself with certain issues.

❖

CHAPTER 43

Love of Travelling

Relocation and Enriched Education

This is a change of location or residence from one place to another; either for a visit or for a stay. It is commonly said that "travelling is a part of education". It gives you a knowledge and experience of what is happening on the other side of the world. It makes you familiar to other places and thereby have more friends from different places collectively. Travel broadens your knowledge and advances to maturity with experience.

There are so many purposes of changing one's place for another by travelling. In search for a job opportunity can make someone to change present place of being for another. Something must definitely warrant whereby a man has to change his or her location.

Relocating is of different reasons. Searching for a greener pasture is very vital whereby your place is not really economically buoyant enough. There could be a case that involves someone has to travel across the seashore even to the Western part of the world in order to copy ideas from the white races. It could be through education by practical and theory or in practice only. It challenges you to measure up in endeavour. A change of residential place for another can add value to your person. You can also travel because you want to enjoy infrastructural facilities at a higher level.

Many Reasons to Escape

Many people leave their respective places, local governments, states, and countries, for another as a result of being declared wanted criminals, assassins, ritualists, kidnappers, a bad business person and so on. Shy could stimulates interest in travelling in order to change residence due to being confessed a notorious witch or wizard. When he or she commits a heinous crime of a great omen, which can bring calamity that will result the guilty being used for a sacrifice to appease the mind of the gods and the only solution is to evade from the land for a safer place, it can occur.

Changing of location can warrant by an individual when he or she will have over used his house for a naughty business which may result arrest in the nearest future; peradventure the secrets link. For instance, a fellow murdered someone in his or her house, and so the only way to conceal without being caught is to exit as possible.

Such a one can even leave without taking a pin in the house. Fear of discovered pestilence or muster existing in the house even after being ventilated can make someone to change environment. If you are an informant to the police, you can be forced to relocate for a possible safer place according to you. This is because putting yourself in a shoe that you just can't continue to relate, could backfire somedays whereby you are expected to; as bargained in the first place.

Avoiding Jail

You might just risk jail if you don't change environment. People with some histories of certain problems of spiritual threats can so feared with assumption that their places could possibly be known by some of their relatives thus, changing of residence can birth a sort of alternate means to avert the whole suspicions.

Have you ever come out of your shell for another, even for just a short period of time? If yes, only you are the best person that still can explain the whole lot of your observations and experiences. Keep it to yourself for that is your personal privacy no matter the content of the whole thing. That is exactly what I'm talking about. It makes you know that water has different types. Atmosphere is of varieties. Breeze has different types as well as due.

❖

CHAPTER 44

Love of Power

Intoxicates

Power is the physical and mental ability put to effect production; whether sport, job, advice, communication etc. It is the strength with which every living thing uses in moving about in search for a daily bread. Everyone likes it. It is very good when it goes with wisdom and ability.

Unfortunately, it intoxicates those that lack the ability: wisdom to control it. And if care is not taken, it becomes even a power tussle; by using violent to live with people around them. Looking at others so very little or be little others in everything is something else. One needs to check what is really wrong in that circle. They so much believe in getting their freedom this way. Even though it might just embrace a kind of fierce appearance, look, it is never the yardstick measure for a total freedom.

Certainly, some people might really get scared of you but at a time it will occur to their understanding that you just can't beat everybody. Maybe you put on this arrogant attitude for a defence of both self and people around you and if not checked it can spoil a lot. It depends on how you are able to regulate yourself on the basis of drawing with or and some people closer to yourself; else, you risk losing even friends along with just ordinary people. The simple fact is that, humans are even hard to get along with, not to talk of scaring them away and at the same time would also want to have them back.

Different Types of Power

We have different types of powers. One, natural power and this is subdivided into gifts and natural powers. This is the degree of a certain abilities, which the Lord God has allowed to form along with a particular body of an individual personality from the very womb of the mother. Samson was naturally gifted power by the Almighty God right from the womb of the mother, in order to defend the people of Israel.

Today we call such element a one man squared. A champion or a giant. Due to the fact that this was a special gift from the Lord, it therefore has certain prohibitions to guard and maintain. In other words, there were some does and don'ts; failure to obey would result in disaster (Jgs 13:5).

Evil Power

Secondly, evil power: Satan the devil is very good in coping God eventually in everything. He can also make some evil spirit to possess some people in order to empower them extra ordinarily just to do a job of evil mission for him. Similarly, he could make native doctors to assist some elements with some diabolical power in order to facilitate crimes with fearlessness.

Artificial Power

Artificial power is known as power-up. Some elements feel that taking hard drugs or smoking marijuana is the best. Really, it heightens their natural power but after sometime it begins to go down. There is no way diminishing return would not set in anything being consumed or rather taken to excess. Some people use it to do sport like wrestling and sex films. There are various motives for this. It could be with a purpose or a competition to win a prize or better still the fellow just want to break record as an ultimate human on that basis.

Reactions can make so many people embark on taking hard-drugs in order to defend and rescue a victim. You see, to be able to withstand opposition by either charting or dragging and retaining a position one claims to defend, it may just be humanly required. As he or she wants to be above rivals, an additional power is necessary. Power sometimes when it couples with certain authority and if not being put under control can result in a dictatorship and autocracy; he or she might even become tussle.

Allurement and Addiction

This is because not all powers equate with the degree of element of senses one has in one's upstairs and as such, who knows, it might just go out of control. When you keep company with who believes in artificial power, he or she may just lure you to be a party to his allurement. And you will be come addicted to it at the long run if care is not taken. For your information, anything more than the natural power, which you are endowed with by God is detriment and can fail you at any time.

Be careful how you apply new things into your lives and systems. Many have incurred damages as a result of these attempts. The natural and the artificial hardly harmonise as one would assume to be the result or outcome. All bloods do not have the same receptiveness.

❖

CHAPTER 45

Love of Performance

Popular Entertainment

This is the display of what someone can do best. It varies simply from individual to individual, due to grades in persons. And that of course will take us to categories of persons. Upper, middle and lower classes, as sets of human beings that do exist in the world. In the upper class, you have the stars: presidents, and others political figures. In royal leaderships you have the kings and the queens. In sports and movies, you got the footballers, wrestlers and others. Actors and actresses, musical artists, adventurers and inventors even the directors of organisations, etc.

Owing to their positions and works in our society, people pay even money to watch them as audience or as spectators any time the need arises. Whenever they are performing their entertainment, their fans almost run crazy for them. You can imagine how billions of people patronise just an album produced by a musical artist.

This makes them so very famous in our society. They are popular because they are well known worldwide. Through gadgets and other devices, social media agents do help in the spreading of their performances and existence to the world to get to know that such people exist somewhere around the world. Really, such publications do go viral. I tell you. This is simply carried out with all carefulness in order to create awareness. whether or not being sent as a specific delegate. Your level of doings and capacity in your belonged career can award you with certain commendations.

Competition

In performance. sometimes we have competition, which might likely make a person want to be the ultimate best of all and if possible to even break records. If you want others to envy you for good, you must let your doings speak for you, by measuring up in your performance; in that you can obtain such credit. This is quite obvious when different artists are called to perform live on stage. Audiences can judge their performance without being asked to.

Their eyes have seen something and so, mouth must therefore express the point of view and what is felt generally. To press observation, which is so impressive, (catching and funny), it is an errand people can go to even without being sent.

In professions, which are the middle class, like the professors advocates and others try ways possible to turn up excellent vivid services to whomever is concerned. Your level of knowledge and skills are what mostly determine here. Some of the rich people do show-up just to let public know that they have improved in standard of living. They help people in order to exhibit their human motive just to be known and popular among human beings. Your career and wealth could make you popular anyway. And of course, even yield you with many known and unknown friends you can't just count.

This is more than just possible as many would want to identify with a notable figure in our society. Their human influence alone can yield many with positive advantages by your side. I thank God that present era has advanced to computer age. So, you connect to be connected and love and be loved through mail or website on the internet.

Yearning for Recognition

Social media had positioned people in such away that almost everybody is equal in the system. When you are a wise person, people delight in your doings. Mostly when the wisdom is from the Lord God Almighty. King Solomon was recognised during his time, in that his fellow kings and queens would come from far and near to listen to the words of wisdom of God through him (1 Kgs 4:34).

Perhaps, the popular performance almost everyone is yearning for, is the ability to satisfy one's opposite in the closets in bed of action. I tell you, so many people even go as far as using all kinds of medicines: orthodox and tradition; for example that which is either for enlargement or developing a big size of one's privates or even a bit longer in order to be able to play as much as possible, just to increase satisfaction it can render to the concerned and as well as to whom it plays. Moreover, the time spent on it: the durability is also considered.

Excessive Reproduction

Some even want to even show-off in the area of reproduction, to show that they are more active and functioning than others. The fact that you are so very prolific does not give you a show guarantee; which can pose even a challenge on others. Forgetting that if one over reproduces (without the necessary requirements to cater for them), one may suffer with them.

The question is when should one really stop? Well, the answer is not far fetch. Economy should speak to you even better, based on the world system as at present. If you weigh yourself so very well with the prerequisite and you feel you are capable, no problem because, you got your life. A man with his home.

❖

CHAPTER 46

Love of Male/Female Privates

No Special Lessons Required

Sincerely speaking, the Lord God has given every sex organ, each as far as human beings are concerned. The purpose is to enable or enhance reproduction and some discharges. They both function naturally without special lessons behind them. For example, you don't teach a child to urinate, only to avoid doing it at home or on clothing; not how it comes out.

You don't teach or lecture a child how to sweat. How to pass some waste-product are never taught but to avoid doing it in a wrong place and on clothes. For example, a fellow will only attain the age of puberty and then just begin to find him or herself reasoning some how pertaining to sex, with his or her opposite sex. Surprisingly, when he or she sets eyes on his opposite sex, some feelings of sensations go down right inside of him or her, which has to do with intercourse.

In eulogy, I discovered that there is this particular object among the references, which even when it doesn't look for trouble, yet trouble must find it out. It always remains calm, cool, soft, kind, meek, gentle, obedient, and respectful yet, the possessor always betrays it when the need arises. To the extent, everybody beats the hell out of it and mercilessly leaves it half dead, including the owner, even without a cause or cogent reason. Some will give their own for about fifty to hundred people, to beat a day, yet continue the following day with the same pattern. Why? May God help the prostitutes.

Natural Urges

Urges are simply natural. Even though there could be sometimes abnormality as a result of other influence or interference. Powers can influence a situation like that. But my discussion is centred now on the positive kind of urge. Although, the Lord God has given us power to put them into control. And if it goes beyond control of an individual, it can then result lust and that of course if care is not taken could produce negative result.

The devil can use it to battle against anybody, whose weak-point is relatively close to this, just to fall the fellow from his or her position. If you have tasted the sweetness, you would want to reach the final bus-stop of which there is even no one. That is to tell you actually, that "the journey of the vagina is a complete long gate." The only thing is that you will wear yourself down and then resign to using power-up. For your information, there is no artificial product without an expiry date.

Artificial Enhancements

The striving to be man enough before a woman in bed has made so many guys or men to go into searching for pills in order to develop their penises that is to enlarge or extend its length because they just want to get their maximum utility or satisfaction from ladies and as well as to satisfy them. The same notion is what makes them to want to spend more than enough time on it. Some bad guys do it too; by taking hard drugs in order to be able to sexually punish any of their targeted ladies for a punishment due to her offence against them in the past.

Naturally, a man or a guy can be lucky to have it given to him naturally by God. Therefore, such a one does not have to go for any place for an artificial enlargement or even extra length, beyond what's natural. It can as well determine by the using of power-up by the fellow in question or even enhance by the negative side of the world meanwhile lies with a mission underneath.

Fashion is an easy process, which lures people into making some elements to start eating what will make them to be able to develop their privates. As for the ladies, they do pump their own also. If you have been moving with a guy, and he is the type on this side of life, gradually one day, his doing might just even influence or lure you into it.

There are people who do not like sex too much, but when they are mistakenly trained, they become mad for it. A little wander why?

Demonic Influence

Demons are sometimes responsible for why some people's demand for sex is excessively more than normal. It can make the victims sleep around or even rape or fret. And so, whatever that fellow will be doing pertaining to sex will be extra ordinary; excessive due to regular practice. This set of people hardly get satisfied with just one person, owing to this, their relationships or marriages do not usually last. In most cases, Satan uses it as an attack against couples that do not have faith for each other. The moment each of them tests the other out there, they become morally loose in that aspect.

Some pump their penises and vaginas, in order to get attracted by their opposite sex. And that takes us to the causes why the yearning for extra large and extra length a kind of desirable sizes by an individual at a particular point in time. As there is nothing that happen on this planet which has no base or even a foundation and we all know that in the spiritual realm, manipulations do take place in order to see if physical could be put under control. In the realm of the bad spiritual world, the concerned people do make their choices based on their desires or wants.

Beyond Normalcy

For example, a fellow or guy could decide to possess an extra large or long penis just to be able to get the lady or woman fully satisfied and as well as to obtain or even extract his own. But it is a pity that no one has ever and will ever attain extremism because it is unattainable.

Beyond normalcy could result in one taking artificial means to heighten their natural limit in order to achieve it, yet up to no avail because it must return to a natural state no matter what. Or as an instrument of Satan, the devil specifically projects to feed on the eggs of ladies, which is usually carried out intelligently for money rituals; or power for more missions.

Fornication and Bisexuality

Similar thing is applicable to ladies with an extra vagina with clitoris. You will be surprised to see a fellow with extra ordinary beauty, shape and attractive appearance. No eyes will ever pass you by without a second look. And there is always a problem with a second look; believe it or not. And that of course must flash some feelings usually unspeakable to your mind.

That is what the bible treats as, fornicating with the mind. Before God, it is wholly regarded as a sin. May the good God deliver us. It is because she has been endowed with from the dark world. All these are instruments to turn the world upside down completely. Since it involves money, you now see the interested sets of people doing blue-films. When they will have gone far and fed up with ladies, they will decide to give themselves to try being bisexual.

Note, if a guy you do see on regular basis suddenly changes shape, mostly on the bottom and it has started to rise with a change in movement, you must know that something is fishy somewhere.

An Over Fascination with Money

It is actually a bad societal programme, which is some how compulsory for the members. Either for security reasons or for semi-holiness. When partners are not also on good terms with the law of operation, by all means to protect yourself against an inexplicable dye, which has already been cast and may definitely be the order of the day. Some men also do in order to protect their partners and families, including children.

Why all this? An over fascination with money of course. And in view of this fact, you find out that it is not really the fault of some people. If you trace their origin, you discover that they are cursed. Such people are just operating under a curse on their lives. Take a glimpse at something, because overlooking can develop room for access.

One of the gifts of females is attraction and if you are the type who is so very much curious about the content of every beautiful thing, behold, you might just be ensnared by one someday. The popular saying: "Something must kill a man," actually emerged from this perspective. The devil can never tempt with what is not so very important to an individual personality. And many times, trials befall you with the calculation of trapping you, if not to totally eliminate you.

The majority are held captive on this basis. This is because so many people like grooving and the high-life.

And you and I know that high-life is incomplete without ladies: instruments of Satanic destruction. Since the devil has devised that man is naturally born with sugar, he now decides to strategically design his method through this process to get people for himself.

Sugar with no education should be put under control, if not all the negativities it contains, when consumed in excess, would be checked. Natural desire in you, couples with other negative influences egging you, in order to posse you with stress up to the level of a huge gravity at this point, you must require Almighty God to help you out if you don't want to surrender.

Satanic Destiny & Avoiding Temptations

There could be Satanic destiny, which cuts across the process of having to go through there. As you have no choice, therefore on arrival there you must do what they do, except you just want trouble, which I presumed you don't. Sickness could result in an abnormal swelling of the privates. Some outfits make it even more pronounced and thereby make whoever that sees it to begin to grasp some messages you are trying to pass across.

Clothes define a fellow of what he or she does and where he belongs. In some clubs, ladies dance naked and that ministers some attractions to the viewers. Moreover, it depends on your level of interest in sex (either at a higher/ lower level or rate). Actually, there are some sexual helpers that prefer it excessively.

For this reason, your mentality must switch by force. Information about innovation on sexing could ring your brain into thinking otherwise, on how to embark on it in order to give it a try. And it could then be a kind of set-up for that fellow and at the end of the day, he or she now falls victim if care is not taken. If you can't beat temptations don't even make attempt to go to where you will come across them. Prevention is better than a cure.

❖

CHAPTER 47

Love of Flowers

To Freshen the Atmosphere

Flowers are the beautiful part of any plant from which fruits are developed. It adds colour and fragrance to nature and thereby renders the atmosphere more fresh. Except one is allergic, one really needs to enjoy the benefit of a flowering atmosphere. It is a symbol of love, for both the dead and the living, among the human race.

Symbolically, many people prefer that you buy them flowers to express and demonstrate your love for them. It makes them feel highly honoured to be presented with flowers, when occasion calls for it.

Instead when you are engaging with your fiancée, preferably seal the covenant up by flowers, with a written note, which comprises a few words of love. To tell your date how much you feel for her.

Flowers are used in so many ways. They add colour and beauty to the compound in which they are planted. Economically, flowers are put into various uses. So many types of perfume are made of flowers. You can process them in order to get different types of oil from them; for cooking and for creams. Almost all fabrics are designed and coloured by the pictures of flowers.

Some clothe dyes are products made from flowers, which attract attention due its beautiful appearance. Also breads are baked with flowers. You have so much nutrients, which you get as a result of consuming any foods made from flowers like: fats, carbohydrates and oil.

Employment Opportunities

Flowers provide employment opportunities too, since companies who deal with flowers (as raw material), require more than just a single labourer; rather so many labours are needed. Finally, it contributes its quota to the global economy. Spiritually speaking, when you dream and see flowers, it denotes that you are in your attractive age, with love all around you, especially if you are a girl. And flowers in the morning, makes you even more beautiful.

When the sun beats down, flowers dwindle and fall, especially in the evening. Meaning, a lady has her years of attraction and that is her right time for marriage and the moment it passes, it is late already. Thank God for His Word of grace over rusticated situations. Otherwise, it would have been a total misery. I mean a cataclysmic finish.

We have different types of flowers such as roses, sunflowers and many more. Economically, flowers can be used to process perfumes, colours and dyes. They have natural beauty to give to lovers. Until tomorrow, the government in the Western world spends huge sums of money on flowers, in order to add beauty and colour to their cities. We all say well-done to all the horticultural experts.

❖

CHAPTER 48

Love of Fashion

Meeting Modern Requirements

Fashion is a form of imitation with which anyone can participate. The modern era has embraced fashion, so much so, that if you are not a party to it, you feel dejected by society. Fashion is useless when you do not have money. A prostitute will only get attracted when she is always cleaned up with quality and good looking outfits. That is to tell you that it takes a whole lot of money to be able to meet up with these conditions.

When we mean clothes, we don't just mean wrapper. It is one thing to get your requisite and another thing is to have the wisdom or knowledge to use it. If you have clothes, but don't know how to wear or use them, in proper order, it can never yield you with certain respect. And it is the equivalent to not having any at all.

There are different types of clothes in the global world. They are divided into tradition and English clothes. Your wearing of traditional attire with all kinds of corresponding shoes or sandals, are only suitable for occasions like native weddings, naming ceremony, cultural dance, baby dedications and more. If you are representing any chief on any occasion, you are expected to demonstrate with the appropriate attire.

The black-races are mostly concerned with these fabrics, which portray tradition and the cultural heritage of the people. English clothes, in short, are more or less suitable for all races. Suit jeans are mostly used by all classes and races. Jeans in most cases do go with canvas, sandals, palm-slippers and fine shirts or tops. While suits go with quality shoes along with good long or short-sleeves, plus a tie for men, including a good belt and a quality wrist-watch.

Fashion & Cars

Mobility is a part of fashion. Cars attract dignity and personality among the human race. Cars are a choice anyway. A choice in the sense, there are people that have money but lack the interest in buying cars for their private use. They can buy, but just do not want to.

There are many reasons behind that, which I will leave for you to sort out yourself. There are different types of cars. Money and choice will determine as to which type of car one is to buy at a particular point in time. People who are not vigilant take every person riding in cars to be a rich, so resign themselves to thinking these are the right ones for dating or even marriage. In fact many have married simply because of fashion.

Single Ladies don't be so Desperate

Such mentality doesn't help anybody nor does it go far with whom it's concerned. For a single lady on the ground to guess any single guy to be a right man for a husband is an error. The fact that you are due doesn't mean you should be desperate about it.

The pattern of houses built by some personalities are as a result of imitations; just as every other thing embraces the latest season. Some because of this sold their old houses for a new one, which is either bought or built afresh; just to blend with the fashion.

Remember, too much fashion could give you extra-large shoes, which can in no doubt slow you down. Some have even used their old houses to do rubbish and then run to buy a new one for safety purpose. Gotten the measure which they have humanly taken so far may not be a complete guarantee for their actual suppose safety. Nature has a boomerang one cannot escape.

You can't kill your fellow human being in your old house and then run for a new one and even expect to be saved. You can't use your old house to sell cocaine and expect to be freed from the new one. It is you that needs to change and amend your ways for good. It is not a question of changing your environment; rather a change of heart that reflects a genuine repentance.

The Evil that Men do Lives with Them

Some have used their homes as a store for the kidnaping of children. May the Lord God deliver you people. If you used your home for a hotel, what assurance have you that something will not happen to that house even you in the nearest future. The evil that men do, lives with them.

Some people embark on travelling abroad usually either by land, sea or air; with a purpose just to make sure they meet up with the challenges their peers posed on them. This you can agree with me is nothing but a complete fashion. You don't imitate in doing anything in that regard.

Fashion can land you in trouble. It is likely that you never sent any act of intimidation. One thing someone forgets to realise is that abroad is not meant for everybody. Cut-throat acquisitions can mislead you if not properly checked or handled.

Being over ambitious is a misguidance. Influence of that circle is so high that you need to deliver yourself before even you regret your action and decision. If you because of any fellow involve in any business transaction you are not too good in and at the long run, when you can't just do well, your yearning will automatically develop into enmity.

If you try to behave exactly like your fellow human beings, the difference will always be there. It is quite obvious that imitation and nature are quite different things all together. And if care is not taken, you might just end up coping the wrong character and thereby begin to fight people on the street like the street obtuse as do some of the junkies, drunks, even the mad people and worst of all, you become violent.

Violence is Part of Lawlessness

A fellow maybe cool and gentle but because of his or her friend is involved in riot, he will be forced to join with them and that maybe the end. Couples could be unfaithful to each other as a result of wrong association. However smart and intelligent one may likely be in copying characters, one just can't change one's voice.

People, your lives matters so very much. If you welcome wrong associates you are a going where only God can deliver you. Who are your close friends in the business circle? Who are your close friends in the job circle? Who are your close friends in school? Besides the tie of brotherhood in the church of Christ as one collective members — body of Christ, who are your friends? Be informed that people have been jailed due to companions. People have run at a loss in the various businesses due to wrong involvements. There is associational influence take care you don't get yourself hurt even before you get to realise it.

Musical artists can imitate one another in songs, in lyrics, rhythms, tones and even sounds yet the difference is still very much cleared. Albums and beating could look very much alike, voice will always define a particular singer at every point in time.

Church is not a Fashion Club

Some people select places and whom to marry as a result of their friend choices. As it favoured their friends they would assume with the belief that it will as well favour them for real. Assumption is never in anyway a complete original measure for judging anything. It is a notion so baseless that you just can't have a concrete info to grasp its meaning and direction.

So many churches are opened due to fashion; get me right I am not castigating but it is a fact. Some pastors plan programmes based on competition and fashion. The fact that the members keep you worried that if you don't do certain programs doesn't mean that you must do one by force. It is not a club. You don't hold the faith of our Lord Jesus Christ in respect of any man. God is not a joker. I pray someone should understand what I am trying to marshal out here. God blesses you if you do understand.

All students are not supposed to study the same course. Imagine a student can decide to change school because of his or her friend. The problem is that whom you waited for may not even have your time as a bosom friend would.

The Dangers of Imitation

If an opportunity comes their way they dash into thin air and that is the end. Can you follow them everywhere? Professions are fashioned in this world. If you follow a habitual smoker too much (with a claim that you can't change or influence them), then there is every tendency that they must influence you, sooner or later. You may even be the one who ends up joining them for a smoke. Same with those who drink and abuse alcoholic beverages defiantly, you will one day blend-up just to keep them happy and retain your friendship.

Not all rebels and criminals are really or naturally born; some are incurred by fashion. Whatever you do, I advise therefore you take care so that you don't harm yourself by imitation. In fashion, there are some clothes, specifically meant and designed for special occasion.

For example, clothes for clubs, cooks, night-gowns, indoor stabilisation of love clothes, marriage clothes or wedding gowns, ordinary party clothes, working clothes, yet some people are ignorant to these and as a result end up muddling everything up and then begin to fool themselves around even before the public. Dressing half naked doesn't usually attract you with original love. Covered foods are delighted by real original men.

❖

CHAPTER 49

Love of Skin Colour

Self Maintenance

It is nature that tells whether you were born beautiful/handsome or not. Although, nobody is ugly and nobody is too beautiful. God cannot give you skin and start bathing you up everyday. It is not God's duty to do that. It is not possible. You are to do the maintenance yourself.

Again, your ability to maintain self determines your level of attainment; just as an illiterate cannot expect PhD degree in their letterbox. Beauty/handsomeness could put you in trouble just to tell you that some beautiful things attract disadvantages also.

Sometimes, God can look even at your destiny and decide to reserve a part of your beauty or handsomeness for security purpose. But if peradventure you are ridiculed to scorn and it annoys God, He would bust you the rest just to tell you that look, you got extra you were reserved for and there is nothing He—God cannot do (Jer 32:27).

Your Skin Reveals how Healthy you Are

Beauty or handsomeness is a trait of an individual, which is likely to be inherited from both parents or one among the two. Your skin colour is not determine by the quality of cream and the corresponding oils with which it is mixed; rather, it simply goes beyond that. Many at times, some of us do complain of a less shining skin colour. Let me tell you, have you taken a proper care of your (inner) self or system first by learning to feed adequately on good food?

Wrong foods or wrong stuffs can always give a complete wrong result, even sickness. If you do not balance up your diet on your daily food intake, forget it. Look, what we consider to be enough stuff, is not even sufficient to match in order to give your required nutrients in the body when critically analysed.

For example, if you are sick, do you start wearing lace? I think you should treat yourself first, before even thinking of dress and look good, descent and elegantly in your outfit. This is because, what is in the clothes is what really matters, not the clothes themselves. As your pores need to breath freely, perfectly and regularly as when due and necessary. A healthy person is known from the skin and as well as how he or she breaths. If you are poor, dirty even feed on anyhow food, skin will testify against you for real. As we all know that wrong appearance is abhorred by men.

Medically, we've been guided with some instructions like: you and your kind of foods, clothes, bathroom and bathing, bedroom, sitting-room, kitchen, toilet, environment, etc. and any other ones can be taken care of by the doctors if need be.

If you are really nourished, you yourself will confirm it yes you are done with the care you actually give to yourself. Beauty has made some modern people to resign to panting their facial look in order to suit their kind of desirable supposed look by a reflection as if it is just as easy as they think just like that. Whatever you are as an individual, you are already, you can't change it no matter your effort to effect any change maybe put in place. I can only advise you to maintain the level you exited with rather than striving to feature with other's . It just can't work. Only your Creator knows why; it's unarguable.

❖

CHAPTER 50

Love of Economisation

Minimise Spending & Maximise Income

However wealthy you may be, you still need wisdom to scrimp your resources or else you soon become a debtor. Really, modern technologists are busy everyday inventing the latest products. Sometimes, if you trust yourself, do forfeit some of them for simplicity. That is part of the wisdom of living.

Nations, families, individuals and companies, need this ability to utilise resources in order to minimise spendings and maximise income. You must never buy everything by sight; no never. It is not good. It is never in anyway a good agility. It is rather a whole lot of crazy fashion. May God deliver someone.

Companies can sometimes plough back profits for a future expansion of a business. You don't just consume all you realise instead you are expected to save part of your stipends or income or even profit. That serves as your saviour if the business should flop or no job for a time be. Saving is a part of empowerment to both individual and government.

The Importance of Savings

You can help yourself to ease your standard of living. What you do is to save part of your money for future use. It is advantageous if you have emergency like unforeseen circumstances and buying of quality products with high discount. Apart from that, it enhances your resources, income or profit. Even though it doesn't entail any kind of competition, yet it is compulsory, you do the correct thing and then enjoy the best. It is a self voluntary decision to do. And when carefully respected, it is simply just like a principle it will definitely be a great help to you in the nearest future.

Only the grace of the Lord God can actually help an individual to scrimp. Resources have war battling it, in order to be very scarce in the hand of the supposed personality at a particular point in time. May the good God help us. Certain powers could bewitch any targeted victim just to make them lose guard.

Before he knows it, extra spendings become his or her practices. Not until the money is finished he may not remember what he was supposed to do with it. Good plans can elude when cash is at hand/in account. The moment it is finished you see the victim become so loaded with plans but this time around no power or resources to follow it up. Many have been influenced to lavish money worth to build homes for irrelevant things. What a life! Only God can explain the mysteries lie in this circle I try a kind of explanation to our understanding. May God help His people.

If you manage to have one house, more than the worth of that house is being wasted on women. It is being wasted on an irrelevant charity you weren't appreciated. At a time you began to blame even yourself whether charm was being used on you or you were under compulsion of something. May God deliver us. Many are puzzled on recalled with some encountered that never yielded any positive return income; only for you to waste your whole lot of sweat, energy, plan in the whole systems.

Some people are ungrateful even though our benevolence is to God the rewarder of the secret good we all carry out to do to our neighbours. May His name be praised. Sorry for the series of activities and holidays enjoyment you have sponsored without even a common thank you from the beneficiaries.

❖

CHAPTER 51

Love of Festivity and Holidays

Celebration

Annually, people celebrate all kinds of invents or celebrities to express their achievements or success over one or two things. A king or a queen can celebrate his or her anniversary with the subjects just to express his happiness and also to enjoy some merriment. The warriors do celebrate their victory after a long war with their enemies. The Christians celebrate Christmas every 25th December yearly in order to express the commemoration of the birthday of Jesus Christ: the Anointed Saviour as the saints have programmed it, even though it was not the exact date of birth of Jesus.

During these periods, nobody goes to work nor travel anywhere for a reason outside this. And that doesn't mean the naughty business personalities do not embark on their business trip on that day. As that could be their relatively safer opportunity to travel freely in order to beat the law with a camouflage, wishes of Merry Christmas. It is a time one relaxes and give the Lord God a big thank you. There are other festivities apart from Christmas, which make the government to observe the holidays so that people can comfortably relax and celebrate it with their families, loved ones and friends.

Individually, we do celebrate feast at times. Feasts like traditions and English festivals are part of our systems of living due to cultural heritages. As you can see, there is so much stress in life. The nature of mankind has become a thing of life, which is a whole lot of battles. And as such, it is therefore advisable that one should endeavour to mix one's stress and problems encountered sometimes with at least certain enjoyment in order to make oneself happily relaxed and even comfortable. If you can't make yourself happy, no one out there will make you happy.

The truth is that there's no special time or specific time for enjoyment. And so, enjoy wherever you are. You can apart from that also travel during holidays to catch fun and also to have good time with your family and friends. The simple fact is that he or she does not even know where on earth to start from. This is because he or she cannot know it all nor what you conceal up as an untold problem right inside of you. "Clothes they say cover nakedness".

There are so much in the act of festivity. If you are not a Christian you may not know this. And Christianity has done a great damage to the heart of evil in the world circle as a system under demonic influence. If not for that, the evil ones would say we have swallowed them up. There could be hidden agendas, like rendering sacrifices to the gods the concerned that people believe and worship, based on their religion and culture. And you find now that people still do invite their friends, well wishers and others in this, in order to use the medium to initiate them directly and indirectly into the system.

Since we have been purchased by Christ with blood and we are therefore no longer living for ourselves rather live for Christ (2 Cor 5:15). And that is the more reason we are our brother's keeper to the core on the basis of praying for one another in order for them to make it right with God. You that do not pray selfish prayers, God blesses you; keep it up (Ps 35:27), God blesses you also. Thank you so very much; and once again God blesses. If you neglect, you are a minus.

❖

CHAPTER 52

Love of Insubordination

Lack of Respect

This is a refusal to show some respect to somebody with a higher rank. It is an act of disobedience to orders. For example, couples are meant to come together as one in everything. But surprisingly, or due to lack of respect, the woman decides to open an account, build a house of her own, even with a demand of free entrance and free exit without permission from the husband. Such a woman is full of underrating and lippy against her partner in the ministry of their matrimony. In short she is a rebel.

At this point, the man almost regrets ever being married to her in the first place; due to some percentages of frustration that her doings have posed him. Furthermore, the man is even contemplating whether to file a letter for a divorce. The contempt is humanly unbearable except by the grace of God. He has even noticed some spiritual destructions traced to her by wrecking him off his resources. In short, he doesn't even know if they can still get along together.

Family is our First Ministry

You can imagine in a family, where husbands and wives are working, since the woman doesn't support the man, sometimes food stuffs get scarce in the house because a single hand may not meet up with every need in the home. Despite that, the woman is realising huge sums as her stipends and only knows how to support outsiders, brothers, sisters, parents and friends just to gather reputation that she is so very generous. Reputation is just a glory and one cannot eat glory; that is one thing she must know. I am not saying it is bad to support one's own people and others but let us not neglect our first ministries — our families for the sake of God.

You can't be hungry yet you have to feed people. Feed yourself first even if not unto the fullest, at least to some extent by that you can even see who is truly in need among your siblings and others. And don't forget that a hungry man is an angry man. Besides, who do you think will accept to collect any offer from you with a frank face, even lippy?

Nobody, except an animal, which is not considerate. Rationally, the very first 'dining meal is the eyes of the giver'. If reverse is the case, the beneficiary doesn't care asking you to keep what you have to yourself or rather put whatever you have right in your pocket so that he or she can be for good. Collecting offer from you means a total disarray.

In this case, I would say nothing but that such a woman is an opposition to the success of the man in that challenges or victim. A man you just can't join hand with to raise up for good as a material for everybody in the family, what then is the use of your being married to him in the first place? Do we call that an accident? Of course not.

I simply do believe that your coming together was ordained but only depends on who was responsible. She is a chain of expenses to the very man in question. In the sense, it is the man who will pay for house rent (if he has not built his own house), bills, clothes for both the children and their own. She is the first to laugh at the husband's standard; saying: I don't even know what you are doing with all the money you are making.

Responsible Couples don't Scandalise Each Other

As the man has married, he now has three consecutive families awaiting him for a responsibility, believe it or not. He, the husband, is to pay for the children's school-fees. Yet he has no common peace and comfort in his own home not even for one due to your lippy and nagging.

Are you a wife or a passer by? You can never spoil your company if truly you take it as your belonging place of employment. No one spoils his or her own property nor remains an adamant to the maintenance as well when the need arises. The fact is that no single genuine landlord neglects to take a good care over his property. Responsible couples do not scandalise each other.

Inability to make the secret of their matrimony intact is completely insubordination of them against each other. But one must be the initiator of the whole disaster. If you live with any wrong partner, or girlfriend or even a boyfriend, fiancé or fiancée, permit me to say in that whatever you feed on or eat must be heard by a third party out there.

Two can only move and function together except they are just of the same spirit (Am 3:3). Well, some insubordinations are due to the fact that some men or women have spiritual spouses each respectively. A spiritual dictatorship is a syndrome to a matrimony that yields into it. And such of course is responsible by demonic power. If not so, there won't be any disarray or discrepancy between them.

Bad Advice

Bad friends and bad companies are attackers of good marriages. Owing to bad advices, they can therefore have their mentalities switched into basing their choices on the reactions of both friends and public people. Such advice as: you just want to offer yourself out so very cheap for that good for nothing guy or girl? As elegant as you are one would think that you would be wise to use your common sense not knowing that it is simply not by size nor by height.

Look, I am highly disappointed in you. I don't want to believe that you just big for nothing. Angry baby, is this you? In fact, you have disgraced me and you know what? I disgust you. Whereas, they have no common serious relationship of theirs, which they are even grooming up with a positive hope of a future marriage with guys or men that maybe concerned.

That is to tell you that no single pig wants the other to bath or dwell in a home of the living. They all want to remain in their cultural mound. May the good God deliver us.

Two Rams never Drink from the same Bucket

You see, there is never a time it will ever have been possible for two rams to drink from the same bucket. Just as two kings cannot lead the same kingdom. Two presidents cannot rule the same country or nation in a tenure at the same time. Greed and selfishness are part of the reasons for insubordination. So many people are just too proud with haughty looks, which is written visibly on their faces.

Please, control your ego before things fall apart. Desist from minding their parties before you live your life with anybody you claim to associate or emulate not only in marriage alone but as well as other things. A desire to be praised by men can induce one with such attitudes in between two partnerships. A particular partner would want to cheat on the other in kind and even in business circle; most especially as it has to do with money.

It is a pity for those who cannot put their pride and lust for others into control. If it is by a mistake your partner is found doing what is serving as a question mark in his or her life and if it bothers you, then do something to normalise the situation other than narrating them.

Build him up to your taste; but if on the contrary, it is simply insubordination of you except by finding the other too very rigid above your capacity. It is this same problem that makes people you run things with, to abuse your kind of person on the basis of finance, background, education, marriage, ministry, and reproduction, materials and business and others shouldn't be left in a single hand if two come together as one for a purpose to achieve a goal.

❖

CHAPTER 53

Love of Pride

No Man Prevails by their own Human Strength

This is a haughty look anybody can put on before their fellow human beings or neighbours. It can also be any feeling a fellow can have over success they've achieved by their human effort. The fact that you have been able to acquire wealth, above your equals, doesn't make you the ultimate in the field of success. You just forgot one thing that no man can totally prevail by their own human strength (1 Sm 2:9).

Therefore, if you see anyone in your former lower level, learn to shun it without laughing at the person, remember that they will still overcome just like you. That is to tell you life is never static. The fact that your journey of destiny has some kilometres with gallops. doesn't mean the rest of the road is just like that.

Your Workshop of Destiny

The fact that one is poor today doesn't mean that one will never have to spend tomorrow. Destiny has one character in the sense that what your workshop of destiny teaches you is distinctively different from another fellow's, whose destiny possess another workshop with different lessons also. You must stop any act of castigating and laughing at others.

For example, Ojo is proud of the result of his performance during his exams. The parents are proud of how their children are all doing well in their schools. As no business person will not be proud to see him or herself flourishing in his or her business field.

Unchecked Ego is a Disease

Pride varies, it is either bad or good. Naturally, everyone is born with pride but with power from God to put it under control to the glory of His holy name by nature; so that he or she does not practice it to put us in trouble due to collective responsibility. Unchecked ego is a disease, which has no cure except with total deliverance by God's intervention.

Perhaps, that will take us to the question: "Why are some people over proud? Why do they express their human boast? Why do they attempt to reap their human glory and gratifications even in the position of God?" Answer: They forget that someone created them. It is a complete bewitchment that makes them abuse such a golden opportunity, to enjoy unmerited favour, which money cannot buy. Humanly, before even you choose your style of clothes you love to sow or buy already made, someone invented it and someone has to sow it and above all, the Lord God founded it first.

Why do you exhibit yourself so very proud and brag with it? Keep your ego and put it under your complete control. There were people even before you were born. Whatever you now see, enjoy, acquire, embrace etc., were complete repetitions of what already formally existed. Your case is never a number one in the whole universe.

All Fingers are not Equal

All fingers are not equal. Due to the fact that some are more educated than others, they become so very proud with degree and others whenever they see those that are below their class. A good family background makes certain people to grow and feel very big before others. Let me tell you, reputation is a glory. And you must know that one cannot eat glory. If you don't work to maintain and retain it, it could be a complete parable. May that not be the portion of someone as an audience reading this text right now, in Jesus' name.

Beautiful husband, wife and children are attractive in respect each other. But what a surprise! Is this enough for you to be proud? What about the Creator of everything, including you? What will the holy One of Israel say? You are puffing up with haughty look, simply because you are wearing used clothes, driving a used car, rented or bought an old house? What of those who enjoy them new (when they were just built)?

Ego makes you feel being on top of the world, having and enjoying the above listed material wealth. Not withstanding, you can still take it easy even though you've long waited for it.

Please, enjoy whatever you have and let others be who they are. The contents may actually be pushing you to exhibit or blow up but deny it by simply telling it with no self control. Wealth and acquisitions can intoxicate the possessors, even more than liquor, if care is not taken.

Never Allow Pride to give you Extra Large Shoes

But it is left with you the possessor to tell it that you don't want to disgrace yourself. You must never allow it to give you extra large shoes of a high horse, else to be able to come down and relate with people might just be so very difficult. And if peradventure, reverse become the case, you might just lack the peaceful side to turn your face. Your fellow humans are not fools, rather they are very calculative.

Please, come down from your haughty look. Come down from your high horse. It can't help you. Extra large shoes can easily slow you down even when you tend to smart it up or even conceal it. I am not judging you, neither am I blaming you; rather it is just a piece of advice. I believe and suggest that you should take to be wise. It will definitely be of help to you. Ask God to help you break free from the shackle of human ego, with cage and limitations; God blesses you.

They said money answers all things. Wealth intoxicates the wealthy people or personalities by looking down on others. It is indeed good to have something doing. And so, for this reason, those who are working, tend to intimidate others. Most especially when it is not hard or a dirty job, they always put a smile on their faces, with haughty looks, right inside of them in suits with portfolios in their hands, walking majestically to their various offices.

Human Bravado always looks down on Others

It is a pleasure to have a brother as a governor or even a president of a nation. And so, if care is not taken, his influence could take you up so very high even above your standard and your equals; such that you may even begin to look down on people. More also, if you are over flattered before your arrival in any occasion, whereby you are part of the special guests of honour, your head will grow too big and if not immediately checked, you may just find yourself looking down on others.

At this mood, you just can't make a good speech except you are the intelligent type that can distinguish. If you are the type that tries to always elevate yourself, you may not care and might just end up acting contrarily to what you are naturally fond of.

Natural energy can make someone to develop a kind of human pride of self, by becoming overbold (bravado), looking at others like rats and ants etc.

Authority with uniform is another major characteristic and trigger for pride. For, if they begin to describe you like Mike Tyson, you become very proud. So many police who can't challenge civilians (in the realm of physical combat), due to their uniform — backed up by the legal authority of the federal government—can introduce some irrelevant ill-treatment against people, without any fear of a reaction.

If you dare to retaliate in self defence (defending your rights against law enforcement agents who act contrary to the constitution), you might just be accused of disobeying an officer and immediately be regarded as a lawless fellow who must be punished.

Applied Wisdom stops you from Fooling Yourself

Can anyone beat the government that made law? Of course not, never. But you that use uniform with certain authority by the government should not also forget that it is not the uniform that is on the active actions rather you in the uniform. And so be very careful on how you treat your fellow human beings.

Be distinguished always in your dealings. If you are recruited with your family griefs, or even loaded by a nagging from your wife or even a bulling by your husband, the waywardness of your children, poverty, hardship, anger of your D.P.O., Colleagues in the office, etc., try to absorb it by putting it under control or else if you mistakenly discharge it on the wrong fellow, you will have problem.

Sometimes, an inward anger triggers a wrong action towards an innocent fellow. In that case, you will see yourself later apologising to some other fellows. It is a rash that needed to be put under control with some senses of humour. If you don't apply wisdom in some dealing at times, you may end up fooling yourself.

❖

Ministry Profile

Doctor Agene Justice Onotiemoria (A.J.O.) hails from Uwessan Ibhiolulu, Irrua Essan Central Local Government of Edo State Nigeria. He had his primary education in Uwessan Ibhiolulu, Irrua, his post primary education in Ujabhole Grammar School, Ujabhole, Irrua and Agba Grammar School, Uromi, all in Edo State. A degree holder in Theology from LifeStyle International Christian University, Firenze Italy.

The author is humility personified, kind hearted, soft spoken and cool-headed gentleman to the core. A seasoned writer, a preacher and a pioneer of righteousness. An ordained worker of God's Vineyard as a financial secretary, an usher, a gospel musician, a member of the choir, youth speaker and a deacon. He was formerly a distributor to G.N.L.D. (an Italian company), a civil servant to Bendel Construction Company Limited (B.C.C.L.) Nigeria, and a furniture maker. He is married with a wife and children.

❖

To Contact the Author

Please email:

Agene Justice Onotiemoria
Email: littlejustice508@gmail.com

*Please include your prayer requests
and comments when you write.*

❖

Other Books

**Love
(Love Distinguished - Series One)**

This is a book about Love, in both its negative and positive lights, such as: the love of parents and family, the love of riches and materialism, including the love of patriotism and even unemployment. We will even discuss inappropriate love, such as incest and the use of rituals and so forth.

ISBN: 978-1-909132-28-3, Pages: 244, Format: Paperback, Published: 2023
Also available in eBook format!

**The Wonderland of Love
(Love Distinguished - Series Two)**

This book is the second book in this series; the title being "The Wonderland of Love." I love this concept, as love has many dimensions, covering such topics as Fake and Genuine Love, also in regards to boyfriend, girlfriend, husband, wife and children. The list is endless but a great read.

ISBN: 978-1-909132-30-6, Pages: 272, Format: Paperback, Published: 2023
Also available in eBook format!

Love Distinguished Series

Sweet Bitter Love
(Love Distinguished - Series Four)

Dr. Justice again has put together stimulating truth, saying that you cannot see someone and quickly conclude that they are your bosom friends. In other words, don't be too fast to put your trust or love in those that might turn out to be bitter or sweet.

ISBN: 978-1-909132-83-2, Pages: 246,
Format: Paperback, Published: 2023
Also available in eBook format!

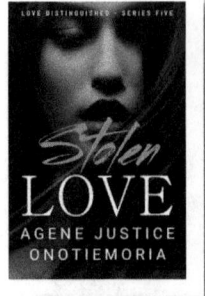

Stolen Love
(Love Distinguished - Series Five)

In this last book of this series, the writer declares that whoever one may be, whatever they do, no matter their race, background, education, class, height, structure, beauty, handsome, rich, poor, barren, married or single or otherwise, they must not allow true love to be distorted or stolen. Remember, all must stand before Him.

ISBN: 978-1-909132-84-9, Pages: 237,
Format: Paperback, Published: 2023
Also available in eBook format!

All Books Available

at

APMI PUBLICATIONS

Email: publications@alanpatemanministries.com
*Also Available from Amazon.com
and other retail outlets.*

www.ingramcontent.com/pod-product-compliance
Lightning Source LLC
Chambersburg PA
CBHW071951040426
42447CB00009B/1308